Praise for *Reboot*

'Jason has set out a vision for business which is more inclusive, engaging and optimistic. This is an important addition to views of the future.'

Martha Lane Fox, Baroness Lane-Fox of Soho

'Theorists like me may have argued for doing business in a way that promotes widespread prosperity instead of extraction, and long-term purpose over short-term profit, but Jason Stockwood is in the trenches showing us all how very possible it is to operate this way. By stressing intrinsic improvement over extrinsic innovation, *Reboot* focuses on how real-world competencies are the key to grounded, sustainable, and socially positive enterprise.'

Douglas Rushkoff, author of *Throwing Rocks at the Google Bus*

'Jason has pulled off a remarkable feat in this book, which crisply articulates the challenges facing the commercial world, by laying out a series of actionable steps that will make the world a better place. As a father of three young children, I hope that other business leaders can also be inspired by his ideas so that we can all help reboot the equation, and create a more compelling vision for the future.'

Peter Jackson, Group CEO, Paddy Power Betfair

'In a world of rapid technological change, companies of all sizes must keep their finger on the pulse in order to remain competitive. *Reboot* is a manual for every business leader to understand what's happening in technology, why, and most importantly, how their companies can leverage each new wave of transformation.'

Pete Flint, Founder, Trulia and NFX

'The acceleration of technologies and the disruption to traditional industries are well documented. How we can address those changes are less obvious. In *Reboot* Jason has tried to demonstrate how business leaders can take a more innovative approach to the tools and methods they can use to ensure their businesses work better for shareholders and for society.'

Brent Hoberman, Chairman/Co-Founder, Founders Factory, Founders Forum and firstminute capital

'Shareholder primacy is the wrong operating system for business. Many of the best, fastest-growing, most forward-looking businesses have realised there is an alternative. They are designing a new operating system that changes everything – from what "leadership" is, to what "employment" means. An operating system that redefines "value" itself. Jason is one of the most successful practitioners of this new operating system, and here he gives a masterclass in it. It is essential reading for anyone who is interested in what will lie behind business success in the future.'

James Perry, Founder, Cook Food & B Lab UK

'Countless pages have been devoted to the story of the technological forces that are inexorably transforming the global business landscape. Stockwood has written the rare book arguing that business leaders have a great deal of choice in shaping how this story will play out. Based on his experience leading tech-driven ventures, his study of the psychology of motivation, and his keen observation of the economic forces driving markets, he shows how leaders can embrace uncertainty, experiment their way to success, and build organisations that thrive by augmenting the abilities of their workers, instead of by exploiting them. I recommend *Reboot* to anyone who is willing to rethink the way businesses are currently run.'

John Beshears, Terrie F. and Bradley M. Bloom Associate Professor of Business Administration, Co-Chair of Behavioral Economics Executive Education Program, Harvard Business School

'This is a very timely, thoughtful and readable book as views on future technologies range from wild optimism to abject fear. The book makes rational arguments about why and how technological advances can be deployed sensibly for wide benefit, to businesses, their employers and customers and to wider society.'

Professor Dame Nancy Rothwell, FRS, FRSB, FMedSci, President & Vice-Chancellor, The University of Manchester

'Read this book and pause for thought. It sets out a vision for business which entrepreneurs can readily sign up to, with a promise of commercial and social gain for many, not the few. Authority comes from it being written by a man who's been there and done it. This has to be on your to-do list.'

Emma Jones, Founder, Enterprise Nation

'Is your business changing at a rate and scale like never before? Are existing norms and best practices increasingly not up to the task of dealing with today's challenges? Then it's time to reboot and I can think of no person better placed to help than Jason Stockwood. Enlightened. Inspiring. And importantly, full of compassion and humanity. *Reboot* is the modern-day playbook for people in business today, who also want to be there tomorrow, too.'

Steve Martin, *New York Times* bestselling author of *Yes! Secrets from the Science of Persuasion*

'At a time where we are debating the future of work and the impact technology will have on jobs, *Reboot* is a timely reminder for us all of our need to revisit our fundamental approach to business and leadership. Jason highlights the need to provide greater autonomy for employees, experimentation and flexibility in order to thrive in the modern age. He showcases how business, if stewarded appropriately, can be a force for good. This requires a shift in our collective focus on the pursuit of short-term shareholder gains to a more long-term sustainable perspective, recognising our collective responsibility to wider society and the environment. "Business as usual" is no longer an option; it's time for a reboot.'

Rajeeb Dey MBE, Founder & CEO, Learnerbly

'An antidote to dystopian and dated ideas about tech and leadership, *Reboot* is a playbook for positive deviance.'

Lea Simpson, Co-founder, Brink

'Jason paints a brilliantly vivid portrait of what a tech business can become when the good of people – whether customers, employees or suppliers – is at the heart of its thinking. It is a story that dispels fear. With disarming frankness he describes his own leadership journey, and celebrates the power of experimentation and the lessons that only come from failing. The hope and excitement the book conveys comes from the lived example of Simply Business, a powerful illustration that there is another way for business to be, apart from the dominant model of the last 40 years. And that business and society can both gain by the creation of highly successful tech business which put, meeting true human needs at the heart of their purpose.'

Charles Wookey, CEO, Blueprint for Better Business

'Packed full of real-world examples and lessons, this book is a must-read for anyone aspiring to be a better business leader and enhance the impact of technology on their business productivity, performance and culture.'

Debbie Wosskow OBE, Co-Founder, AllBright

'In a rapidly changing world, no one has all the answers, but we all need to be thinking about the workforce of the future. Jason Stockwood's voice on the topic is important, and I applaud his innovative thinking and creative approach to experimentation.'

Alan Schnitzer, Chairman and Chief Executive Officer, The Travelers Companies, Inc.

'*Reboot* kickstarts the movement for a positive outlook on change in the practice and meaning of work. Packed full of insight and anecdotes, it's written in the wonderfully authentic voice of a business leader who clearly also has a life.'

MT Rainey OBE, Advertising Founder

RE**BOOT**

A BLUEPRINT
FOR HAPPY,
HUMAN BUSINESS
IN THE
DIGITAL AGE

JASON STOCKWOOD

1 3 5 7 9 10 8 6 4 2

Virgin Books, an imprint of Ebury Publishing,
20 Vauxhall Bridge Road,
London SW1V 2SA

Virgin Books is part of the Penguin Random House group
of companies whose addresses can be found
at global.penguinrandomhouse.com

Penguin
Random House
UK

Grateful acknowledgement is made to the following contributors
for permission to reprint their work: p1 Astro Teller; p47 © Rutger Bregman, 2017,
Utopia for Realists, Bloomsbury Publishing Plc.; p119 © Anne Michaels, 1996,
Fugitive Pieces, Bloomsbury Publishing Plc.; p163
Dov Seidman, p231 © John Berger, 1984, *And Our Faces,
My Heart, Brief as Photos*, Bloomsbury Publishing Plc.

First published by Virgin Books in 2018

www.penguin.co.uk

A CIP catalogue record for this book is
available from the British Library

ISBN 9780753552728

Typeset in 13/16 pt Bembo Std
by Integra Software Services Pvt. Ltd, Pondicherry

Printed and bound in Great Britain by Clays Ltd, Elcograf S.p.A.

Penguin Random House is committed to a sustainable future for our business, our
readers and our planet. This book is made
from Forest Stewardship Council® certified paper.

For Lorna, Bea and Tom.
Love, happiness and sausage rolls.

Contents

Introduction   xiii

Part I: Reboot required   **1**

Chapter 1: A broken model   3
Chapter 2: Under pressure   25

Part II: Rebooting business   **47**

Chapter 3: The question   49
Chapter 4: The answers   70
Chapter 5: The culture   97

Part III: Rebooting leadership   **119**

Chapter 6: Give back control   121
Chapter 7: Take responsibility   142

Part IV: Rebooting work   **163**

Chapter 8: Happy and human   165
Chapter 9: Four days a week   200

Conclusion   219
Acknowledgements   225

INTRODUCTION

SINS OF THE PAST, FEARS OF THE FUTURE

There are two sides to London's Kensington High Street. Above ground is one of the UK's most famous shopping districts, filled with fashion and fine dining, and some of the country's richest real estate. Below ground, 20 years ago, was a room six times the size of the storefront above it: the call centre where I started my career. No windows, no natural light, and certainly no fashionable customers. What we did have was row after row of desks, and from every one of them could be seen an electronic counter, fixed high on the wall above, flashing out in red the number of calls waiting on the line.

How many of those calls you did a day, and how much time you spent at that desk, were the entire world of that job. It was targets as tablets of stone, an entirely fixed working day that was the same every day, and ruled by a management that cared only for the numbers appearing on the screens in their offices. You were either above the line or below it, and that was all that mattered.

It was the first of two real jobs I did in the old world of travel (working at Disney World in Florida and as a holiday rep in Greece were too much fun to be counted as real jobs), before I moved almost completely by chance into the new one, joining lastminute.com at the height of the dotcom boom. This marked my entry into the world of digital business, which over the last 20 years has taken me from travel to dating (Match.com) and finally insurance, in my current role at Simply Business. For a phone operator turned sales rep, lastminute felt like walking into the future, and in some ways it was. The open-plan, flat-hierarchy, wear what you want, and every idea counts approach wouldn't raise any eyebrows now, but in those days it was a revelation. It changed my perception of what a job could be and how a business could be run.

Back then, a new model of work and business was coming into view. Improved technology was starting to make more flexible arrangements possible, and people's desire to be part of rigid company and career structures was waning too. However, almost two decades later, it feels like the brave new world that companies like lastminute paved the way towards has not yet been realised. While many companies have made some superficial moves towards being more modern, democratic and flexible, the core culture in most cases remains hierarchical, shareholder-focused and short-termist. Traditional ideas about how businesses should be run, and for whose benefit, have survived the technological upheaval of the past 20 years with remarkable resilience. The technology may have changed, but those red lights are still flashing away.

Just as concerning as the relative lack of change within the business world is what has changed around it. I walked into the open-plan office of lastminute. com as an unusual hire: I grew up in a northern, council-estate, single-parent home. I never knew my dad, who had walked out on us when I was still a baby, and my mum had to work three jobs to keep us out of the hands of social services, at the same time as raising four boys. I had a brilliant childhood, but did badly at school and went to a university you definitely haven't heard of. My new colleagues mostly went to the two places everyone had. Back then my unusual career path, which began working on the docks in Grimsby at 18, and has ultimately culminated with me becoming the accidental CEO I am today, was made possible by the safety nets that existed in the system: from free higher education to actually affordable housing and stable pensions. I now see very few of those safeguards still in place for young people coming from the same council estates I did. The economic data suggests that real-term wages are stagnating, and many of today's 20- and 30-somethings are on course to be less prosperous than their parents.

In other words, too much of the current business landscape hasn't really changed for the better, and the wider social and economic fabric has probably changed for the worse. These are two problems that are big enough in themselves, and that's before you even get to the looming challenge that means change can no longer be kicked down the road: seismic forces of technological upheaval that are hurtling towards incumbent jobs and business models. When you consider the problems that already exist, and the scale of the challenges that lie ahead, it feels like we have reached an unsustainable juncture. We now face a moment where the sin of the past – an economic model that has produced substantial growth and progress, but distributed those gains far too unevenly – is about to collide with one of the most pressing fears about the future: technological advancement that threatens to wipe out jobs in their tens of millions.

How did we get to this point? It is now close to half a century since a model of doing business that first and foremost organises around shareholders started to become popular. Technology and globalisation have accelerated the effects of that system and revealed its deep flaws: the economic inequality it enshrines, the lack of wider responsibility within business it can engender, and the short-term mindset it often instils. While that system, left on the floor by the shock of the 2008 financial crisis, may just about have risen to its knees in the decade since, its short-comings are now more painfully evident than ever.

If we continue stumbling down the same path, then these problems seem likely to reinforce each other. The budding power of artificial intelligence will lock in and exacerbate the inequalities that the current shareholder-centric system already encourages. The gap between executive pay and average wages will continue to widen; companies will create more wealth for fewer people, supporting a dwindling number of jobs and shouldering a decreasing tax burden. Problems from the pollution of the environment, through carbon emissions and plastic waste, to the health issues that are being caused by a toxic combination of over-work and technological overload, are likely to get worse and not better. Business, which has the power to be one of the great global forces for economic growth, social mobility and positive change, could find itself becoming a catalyst for accelerating prob-lems in society, contributing to the continuing collapse of public trust in institutions and the fissile political climate that we are starting to experience.

That is if things don't change. There is an alterna-tive future, one many in business are ready and willing to help create. If we can re-orient the collective business mindset to be more focused on the long term, more aware of its responsibilities to stakeholders other than shareholders, and more committed to helping people thrive as well as making profits grow, there is an opportunity at hand: not just to build better and more productive companies, but to restore the reputation of business in society as a trusted institution, one that has stronger ties of loyalty with its employees and customers, and which politicians and regulators are minded to support and empower, rather than battle and regulate. That is the reboot I am calling for in this book.

I say this not because I am suggesting that we turn business into something it is not. The instinctive response of some to any argument for a more responsible mode of doing business is to write it off as social enterprise or charity, an erosion of the essential profit motive of capitalism. But it isn't, and to understand why you also have to recognise a less obvious flaw in the current model, beyond its broader socio-economic shortcomings: it doesn't work that well for business either.

As a whole, companies have not seen anything like the overall productivity gains that the technology of the Internet era should have helped create. Many are struggling to reconcile the structural changes that technology is making necessary with deeply ingrained instincts to prioritise the short term. And most are facing the challenge of a disengaged workforce, one in which problems of stress and mental health are getting worse. The current model realises the full potential of neither technology nor people, and while some companies have done extraordinarily well within it, the overall picture suggests a collective level of underperformance. As MIT's Erik Brynjolfsson has said, 'innovation has never been faster, and yet at the same time, we have a falling median income and we have fewer jobs. People are falling behind because technology is advancing so fast and our skills and organisations aren't keeping up.'

We need a reboot in business because it will be good for business, as well as ensuring companies better meet their obligations to their employees and society as a whole. The change I am calling for is about how we can make companies more productive, better able to thrive in an environment of technological change, and happier, more fulfilling places to work. None of this can be achieved without companies and their leaders accepting a broader range of responsibilities: working harder to act in the best interests of their customers, employees and the environment, not simply giving in to the gravitational pull of the bottom line at every opportunity.

Achieving all this will mean a reassessment of some fundamental principles that have governed business and management theory for decades. I will explore issues that include why most companies need to stop talking about innovation, replace the quest for certainty with an embrace of experimentation, and find a new approach to working with technology. I will suggest that the role played by leaders needs in turn to change, and that they must give up much of their accustomed authority if they are to steer their companies success-fully through change and uncertainty. And I will outline how this all needs to be underpinned by a reboot in how we think about and organise work, moving away from the century-old legacy of scientific management to develop a new model that gives people autonomy in, and control over, their working lives. In a business environment defined by uncertainty, I will argue that in order to thrive companies need to become more flexible and less prescriptive in their organisation: light on hierarchy, process and planning, and strong on culture, empowerment and leadership at every level.

The reboot I will explore must stretch across every aspect of how business operates: from how companies prepare for and organise around change, to what they prioritise, how they are led, the responsibilities they take upon themselves and the working environment they create. It is both about fixing problems that are undermining the productivity and perception of business, and how to create a model that can better adapt to the profound technological change that lies ahead.

Technological revolution is the defining feature of this era in business. It is generating huge commercial opportunities, at the same time as challenging companies with the question of how to reinvent legacy business models, and contributing to overwork today as it threatens to create a landscape of substantially fewer jobs in the future.

This ambiguous relationship extends into our personal lives. Technology that was meant to enrich and entertain us increasingly leaves many feeling isolated, bored and addicted. As the academic Laurence Scott, author of *The Four Dimensional Human*, has argued, our digital world has pushed people to a confusing series of junctures: between presence and absence, intimacy and anonymity, involvement and isolation. He writes of the uneasy coexistence of 'cheerful, productive lives amid digital longings and desolations'. In turn social media, which once held the high-minded promise of a global forum of ideas and information, has become a damaging mixture of echo chamber, abuse generator and misinformation factory. 'I think we have created tools that are ripping apart the social fabric of how society works,' the former Facebook VP Chamath Palihapitiya has said. He is just one of a growing chorus of figures from social media's early days who are now warning about the effects of the platforms they helped to build.

Quite simply, technology is not delivering on the promise to make our lives more engaged and fulfilling, our businesses more efficient and productive, and our societies more cohesive and informed. At work and at home, in communities and across borders, it is creating as many problems as it solves. If you want evidence that all is not well, look to the heartland of technology, Silicon Valley, where some of the world's leading entrepreneurs and investors are turning to technology-light schools for their children, and arranging universal basic income pilots to tackle poverty, inequality and housing shortages.

It may ultimately be true, as the futurist Peter Diamandis has argued, that we are headed towards an abundant future, where technological advances will wipe out many of the problems we currently face, making everything from energy to housing, food and transport radically cheaper if not cost-zero. But even by his admission, that is at least 20 to 30 years away, and he is one of the optimists. We need to fix the problems technology has created in the present, and threatens in the immediate future, as much as we look towards the better world it could ultimately build.

How we can reboot our relationship with technology, on both an organisational and individual level, is one of the central questions this book will explore. Technology is often presented as a market force of unstoppable momentum, but companies and their employees are not hostages to its progress. We don't need to buy into the dystopian idea that machine learning and artificial intelligence will destroy work as we know it; and we don't have to let technology dominate our working lives, as many feel has now become the case. There is no reason why technology cannot be used more sparingly, if that helps people to be more productive when at work, and switch off when away from it; or that artificial intelligence cannot be a force to enhance the way people work rather than one that undermines or indeed supplants the human role. We have choices about how we use technology, to what end and to whose benefit. Those choices need to be better recognised than they are currently and exercised more deliberately.

Since my time at lastminute.com, I have been fascinated with how technology is changing the way we work and do business, for better and worse. Over the last eight years, helping build Simply Business from a struggling challenger into the leading UK provider of business insurance, I have experienced both the power of technology to help grow a business and transform an industry, and also become increasingly concerned about how it is affecting us as people. While we have used technology at every turn to try and provide a better service for our customers, we've also looked at how its use should be limited to create a more productive and respectful work environment. With over 500 employees, and nearly half a million business customers, I'm seeing all the time how technology is affecting our own medium-sized business, and the many small companies we serve all across UK and in our US business.

In that time I've gone from running an early-stage venture in the UK to sitting on the operating committee of a US company that's over 160 years old (Travelers, which acquired us in 2017 for $490m), which gives me a new perspective on how a much older and larger business is adapting to these challenges. And I've met countless entrepreneurs and business leaders who I believe are starting to pioneer a better model of doing business, one that's considerably at odds with everything you read about tax avoidance, soaring executive pay and lack of concern for the environment in the business world.

This book outlines my thoughts about how to be a good business leader in a changing world. However, it's also written from the perspective of being a parent (or an aunt, uncle, godparent or mentor) and based on the belief that we can hand on a better world to our children and theirs. If my generation was to give itself a report card at this point, we would have to give the same verdict I used to get on a regular basis at school: 'full of potential, but needs to apply himself'. However, there is time to change that, and no shortage of urgency or opportunity to do so.

I'm going to tell this story not from the standpoint of a technologist or a futurist, but as a simple business builder. What follows is not a template carved in stone; it's a series of ideas, experiences and suggestions on what companies can do to thrive in the uncertainty and upheaval that lies ahead. It's about practical things that any business can seek to implement, based on my experiences of what's worked and, even more importantly, what hasn't. I might not be able to tell you what the future is going to bring for your business, but I hope to provide the guide ropes that will help you experiment your way into it.

PART I

Reboot required

'We can either push back against technological advances or we can acknowledge that humanity has a new challenge: we must rewire our societal tools and institutions so that they will enable us to keep pace.'

Astro Teller, quoted by
Thomas Friedman
Thank You for Being Late

CHAPTER 1

A BROKEN MODEL

How can a business that records an annual loss of $4.5bn be considered the most valuable private company in the world? How can one that sold 76,000 vehicles in a year be worth more than a competitor that shifted almost 10 million in that time? And how could a company that raised almost $930m in funding over its lifetime possibly end up bankrupt?

The companies in question are Uber, whose $68bn paper valuation belies the fact it has never made an annual profit; Tesla, whose market capitalisation in 2017 outstripped that of General Motors despite it being functionally a much smaller company; and Jawbone, a manufacturer of health wearables, which in 2014 was valued at $3.2bn, yet by 2017 had filed for bankruptcy.

They are symptomatic of a corporate system that is going wrong: a market where fortunes fluctuate wildly, and companies are increasingly valued for their ability to attract venture capital and public attention as much as the realities of business performance.

It's a market in which bitcoin, a currency that isn't a currency, can appreciate by 1,800 per cent over the course of one year (2017) and then lose almost half its total value in the next three months. One in which, chasing that same bandwagon, a drinks company (Long Island Ice Tea) can decide it is becoming a technology company (Long Island Blockchain), double its share price overnight, and then see it come crashing down to the point where it is delisted from the stock exchange. A market for companies like Juicero, which took over $130m of investors' money before collapsing under ridicule when it was discovered that the function of its $699 juicing machines could be replicated by hand. For companies like Theranos, whose blood testing technology attracted widespread media and investor acclaim, netting the company a $9bn valuation before the truth was revealed that the supposedly revolutionary devices didn't work, and founder Elizabeth Holmes was indicted on federal fraud charges. Or Powa Technologies in the UK, a mobile 'tagging' business, which claimed a valuation of $2.7bn one year and went bankrupt the next, with its annual revenues never having topped even £5m. It is a market full of false promise and vanity metrics; too many impressive corporate exteriors that ultimately prove to be commercial shells. As the tech commentator Tim O'Reilly has written, many are 'not getting paid by exchanging goods and services with customers, but by persuading investors to give them money'.

You could be forgiven for feeling a bit seasick trying to work out where all that money is going and what the impressively large numbers actually mean. You might equally dismiss all this as nothing more than an elaborate corporate parlour game, where sky-high valuations are traded like Panini stickers, entrepreneurs are heroes one day and villains the next, and there is always a new and more exciting horse around the corner to back.

Except the reality is that market horse-trading and business performance does not exist in isolation, however much of a bubble it might be. Rather it is one of the foundations on which social infrastructure and individual livelihoods ultimately depend, whether that is through employment or the state's ability to raise taxes. We need businesses that provide stable and meaningful employment, sufficient tax revenues to support public services, and which drive innovation that is meaningful rather than frivolous. The true value of a business can only be seen when placed in its wider social context. And it is only by looking beyond the stock market and boardroom, to the impact business has on the world around it, that we can start to understand the true nature of the problem.

Consider, for instance, that real-term wage growth has declined in the UK in every decade since the 1980s, according to the ONS. Or that wages in the US have declined steadily as a proportion of GDP since 1970. It's a picture that, according to the McKinsey Global Institute, extends across the developed world, with the incomes of 540 million people, representing around two thirds of households in the world's 25 most advanced economies, either falling or flatlining between 2005 and 2014.

All told, one of the essential beliefs of a capitalist society – that the next generation will be more prosperous than the last – is under threat. A joint Stanford and Harvard study found that only half of 30-year-olds today earn more than their parents did at an equivalent age, compared to 92 per cent of those born in 1940. The contribution of business to the public finances has also been slipping: while corporation taxes represented almost 4.5 per cent of UK GDP in the mid-1980s, that had fallen to around 2.5 per cent by 2015/16.

These figures are hard to square with the rosy picture at the top of the corporate pyramid. Between 1978 and 2016, CEO pay in large US companies grew by 937 per cent, over 80 times quicker than that of the average worker. In the UK, the CIPD estimates that it would take a worker on the average annual wage approximately 160 years to make what the typical FTSE 100 CEO does in a year.

Some people, and companies, are doing extremely well out of the current system. Wealth is growing and growing, but it's also becoming more concentrated in fewer hands. The richest 1 per cent in America now control 38.6 per cent of wealth, compared to 23.6 per cent in 1980. Internationally that picture is even more extreme: according to a British Parliament

House of Commons Library study, the 1 per cent is on track to control approximately 64 per cent of global wealth by 2030. A similarly Darwinian effect can be seen on the corporate landscape, with the rise of technology behemoths such as Google, Amazon, Facebook and Apple contributing to an existential struggle for industries including media, bricks-and-mortar retail and music.

All of which means our existing model of business is failing to function properly on at least two levels. It's failing as an effective infrastructure to underpin a broad pool of sustainable, job and value-creating enterprises; and it's failing to provide the foundations for an economy in which all can prosper and enjoy rising incomes and standards of living over time.

We did not get to this point by accident. The problems sketched above – from unstable markets to Panglossian valuations and income inequality – have deep roots in a system of doing business that is the product not of a short-term detour, but almost five decades of fundamentally reorienting corporate objectives. To understand what a reboot will look like and how it can be achieved, we need first to understand that system: how it came into being and why it has helped create the problems we now face.

Shareholder gains

To read some of the more lurid tales emerging from Silicon Valley, and follow the more dizzying market rollercoaster rides, you might be forgiven for

thinking that the business world has entered a collective mania: blinded by the possibilities of technology
and the unprecedented pace at which companies
can now grow.

Yet this is no short-term glitch, rather the logical
conclusion of a system that has been developing for
the best part of 50 years. It is the ultimate triumph
of one actor on the business stage, whose role and
interest has been elevated above all others: the
shareholder.

Shareholders form the gravitational core around
which the business world rotates. To a large extent
that is fair and right, because creating value for shareholders is a fundamental part of sustainable commercial success, and it's also easy to forget that many
institutional investors are not the super-rich of cari-
cature, but pension funds representing the interests
of millions of workers whose retirements depend on
their long-term success. The problem is not so much
that business has prioritised the shareholder, but the
extent to which that has been done at the expense
of all others. I know from experience that, when
running a company, you rarely stop thinking about
how you are going to raise money and from whom;
and then, once you have, how you will keep the
confidence of those investors. You soon discover that
managing your shareholders can be as much of a job
as managing your business, and that the needs of the
two don't always dovetail as neatly as you might hope.

So entrenched has the primacy of shareholders
become that it would be easy to assume it has always

been this way, and that the idea of a business as a vehicle for shareholder value is the foundational one. In fact, the shareholder anchorage emerged as a relatively recent, and in its time radical, piece of thinking.

In 1970, the American economist Milton Friedman published an essay in the *New York Times*: 'The social responsibility of business is to increase its profits'. He outlined a view of business that was not just profit-focused, but which viewed any other priority as hostile to that aim. In particular, he struck back hard against the talk of social responsibility, which was popular in the boardrooms of the 1960s as it is starting to become so again today:

When I hear businessmen speak eloquently about the 'social responsibilities of business in a free-enterprise system,' I am reminded of the wonderful line about the Frenchman who discovered at the age of 70 that he had been speaking prose all his life. The businessmen believe that they are defending free enterprise when they declaim that business is not concerned 'merely' with profit but also with promoting desirable 'social' ends; that business has a 'social conscience' and takes seriously its responsibilities for providing employment, eliminating discrimination, avoiding pollution and whatever else may be the catchwords of the contemporary crop of reformers. In fact they are – or would be if they or anyone else took them seriously – preaching pure and unadulterated socialism.

Friedman's essay, and the Chicago School from which it emerged, came to underpin the mainstream of corporate thinking in the decades that followed. It redefined the role of the corporate executive, which, according to his essay, was 'to conduct the business in accordance with [the employer's] desires, which generally will be to make as much money as possible while conforming to the basic rules of the society.'

The Friedman doctrine was more of a departure from the norm than it seems in retrospect. In the post-war years, the focus was generally on stakeholders beyond shareholders, and businesses' responsibility as social organisations as well as profit generators. 'I thought what was good for our country was good for General Motors,' the company's former CEO Charles E. Wilson famously said in 1953, summing up the mid-century spirit of mutuality between corporations and society. Friedman's argument, that such concerns represented a fundamental dereliction of duty on the part of executives, was both a significant departure from the status quo, and a powerful impulse towards a refreshed conception of business around the singular goal of shareholder value.

What began as economic theory has over time shifted into active business practice. As takeover battles raged, institutional investment boomed, and stock options for executives became the norm, the 1980s boom in corporate finance turned companies into more market-driven entities. Shareholder power was seen as the corrective to inefficient, ineffective managerial practices that had created sprawling conglomerates and contributed to a flat decade for investors in the 1970s. Executives were incentivised to think as shareholders by new pay structures built around stock options, and kept in line by the aggressive corporate raiding and takeover culture that flourished.

A ravenous market became the beast that every company and chief executive had to feed in order to survive. And the culture of balancing shareholder needs with those of employees, consumers and wider society gave way to a more blinkered view that made the share price, the quarterly figures and the dividend the first and last priority. 'By the end of the [1990s], any lingering doubt about the purpose of the corporation, or its commitment to various stakeholders, had been resolved,' the University of Michigan's Professor Gerald Davis has written. 'The corporation existed to create shareholder value; other commitments were means to that end.'

In recent years a backlash against the primacy of shareholder value has started to emerge. It has been derided as 'the dumbest idea in the world' by the former General Electric chief executive, Jack Welch, and criticised by a phalanx of influential CEOs including Paul Polman of Unilever, who commented: 'I do not work for the shareholder, to be honest; I work for the consumer.' John Mackey, the founder of Whole Foods Market, has said similarly that 'our most important stakeholder is not our stockholders, it is our customers.' Movements, from Mackey's Conscious Capitalism to B Corp, have sought to give shape and definition to how companies can operate in a way that benefits all their audiences, and indeed society as a whole.

In turn, some academics and lawyers have challenged the consensus that shareholders are the undis-
puted owners of a business, and that directors owe
an overwhelming fiduciary duty to them as a result.
In the words of the late Lynn Stout, then a professor
at Cornell Law School: 'the managers of public
companies have no enforceable legal duty to maximise
shareholder value. Certainly they can choose to
maximise profits; but they can also choose to pursue
any other objective that is not unlawful, including
taking care of employees or suppliers, pleasing
customers, benefiting the community and the broader
society, and preserving and protecting the corporate
entity itself. Shareholder primacy is a managerial
choice – not a legal requirement.'

Furthermore, a legal judgement at the High Court
in 2015, in a case where Lloyds Banking Group was
sued by a group of its shareholders for an alleged
breach in duties relating to the 2008 takeover of
HBOS, confirmed that the primary fiduciary owed
by a director is to the company and not to the shareholders. According to Lord Justice Nugee's judgement,
'in general the directors do not, solely by virtue of
their office of director, owe fiduciary duties to the
shareholders, collectively or individually.' He also
referred to an earlier judgement from Lord Justice
Neuberger in the case of Peskin v Anderson: 'to hold
that a director owed some sort of general fiduciary
duty to shareholders would involve placing an unfair,
unrealistic and uncertain burden on a director, and
would present him frequently with a position where

his duty to shareholders would be in conflict with his undoubted duty to the company.'

Yet while these various critiques have brought some of the problems of the shareholder emphasis into view, the idea remains firmly rooted in mainstream business culture. Companies are obsessional about their share price, anxious about investor moods and disinclined to make long-term investments that might upset the careful balance of their next quarterly report. According to McKinsey, over half of CFOs will reject a promising investment if it means missing their next earnings target, while companies that go public invest almost three times less after their listing than they did beforehand. Its managing partner Dominic Barton – one who should know given the number of FTSE 100 and Fortune 500 firms his company advises – has said that 'most chief executives of public companies in the West feel relentless pressure – from the markets, shareholders and sometimes their own boards – to deliver short-term results. It is very difficult for them to plan long-term investments, even with time frames as limited as three or five years.'

More bluntly, as NYU professor Scott Galloway, one of the most strident critics of Silicon Valley, has said: 'the ratio of 1-per-cent pursuit of shareholder value and 99 per cent the betterment of humanity that technology used to play has been flipped, and now we're totally focused on shareholder value instead of humanity.'

When you are constantly looking over your shoulder at the mood of your investors, second-guessing what they are thinking and how they might respond to some new plan, it is hard to get the clear-sighted, long-term and ambitious perspective that you need to steer a business successfully. As the above statistics show, the unwieldy role and power of investors makes too many companies more anxious and cautious than they should be. Ironically, this may mean that shareholders are undermining their own return, the very foundation on which this widespread reorientation of the corporation has been premised. A study by Roger Martin, former Dean of the Rotman School of Management at the University of Toronto, found that S&P 500 stocks returned an average of 6.4 per cent between 1977 and 2009, lower than the equivalent figure for 1933–76, before the shareholder doctrine began to take hold, when returns averaged 7.6 per cent.

Yet the shareholder-centric model of business is not just broken because it is underperforming financially, or even because of its role in creating the uneven outcomes – at both a corporate and macro-economic level – that I have outlined. At its core, it is broken because it has changed what business believes and how it behaves: enshrining skewed priorities that have created sometimes disastrous results.

Perspective lost

Perhaps the greatest flaw of the shareholder-centric model of business is the myopia it encourages. When you see only the needs of your shareholders, and worship the balance sheet above all else, it becomes easy to lose sight of the many other things that matter to a business, from the wellbeing of employees to the trust of consumers. This loss of perspective can have far-reaching consequences: the evidence of recent decades is that it has encouraged and enabled corporate behaviour ranging from the dangerously optimistic to the downright fraudulent. Of course such malpractice was not invented in 1970: stories of fraud, manipulation and self-delusion are as old as business itself. Yet the examples of the shareholder era suggest a connecting thread: the desire to create magic on the balance sheet, and the stock market, has led companies to grasp at mysterious and often illusory means to justify a short-term end. And generally speaking, what has seemed too good to be true, too perfect a profit-making marvel to be believable, has generally proved to be exactly that.

This was true in the 1990s with Enron, poster child of corporate hubris and market manipulation. What had begun as an energy trading business, taking advantage of deregulation to create a market in energy futures, became a company that sought to repeat the trick in a dizzying range of different markets, from broadband to insurance, advertising and even pulp and paper. Enron morphed into a trading and derivatives jungle that even most of the analysts tasked to it admitted they struggled to understand. At generating hype, devising complex financial instruments and making investments, Enron excelled. Yet it started to fall apart when the journalist Bethany McLean posed a devastatingly simple question in 2001: 'How exactly does Enron make its money?'

On that conundrum, a business that had achieved a peak valuation of $70bn, been voted America's most innovative for six consecutive years, and awarded itself the mantle of 'the world's leading company' rapidly unwound. The truth behind the front was revealed: Enron had been booking loans as profits, recording income that did not yet exist, and hiding debt and toxic assets off its balance sheet. The business that had been too complex for professional analysts to comprehend turned out to be little more than an elaborate confidence trick, one that had sustained itself through the illusion of regular earnings growth, hitching itself to the wagon of the exploding online trading market, and its capacity to create business for investment bankers.

Before Enron became one of corporate history's most compelling cautionary tales, it was one of the world's most admired companies. And its rise and fall cannot be explained without understanding its rigid focus on shareholder value and the share price. As its CFO Andy Fastow, who served a six-year prison sentence for his part in the fraud, recently reflected: 'When I was in business school, there was only one word – shareholder. And I thought what I was doing was good for shareholders and employees, so I thought I was doing my fiduciary duty.'

As Enron was collapsing, another too-good-to-be-true story was developing. In some of the same investment banks that had underwritten its deals, attention was switching to the mortgage market. Through more clever financial engineering – pooling different tranches of risk into single vehicles – banks believed they had created the mechanism to convert risky lending (to subprime mortgage holders) into a stable and lucrative investment proposition, in the form of collateralised debt obligations (CDOs). Only in retrospect can it be so obvious that the alchemy of turning high risk into easy reward was doomed to disastrous failure. The 'financial weapons of mass destruction', as the legendary investor Warren Buffett termed CDOs, duly imploded, helping bring about the global financial crisis of 2008. Once again, disbelief was suspended (and risk managers ignored) because what looked good on the balance sheet and for the share price was deemed to be beyond reproach. Only too late did most banks realise that their balance sheets were holed below the water line, precisely because they had failed to properly scrutinise the products that were primarily responsible for elevating them. Recovery was only possible because governments around the world found hundreds of billions of dollars to rescue them.

It had been a similar story a decade earlier during the dotcom boom, where money and hype flowed unerringly towards companies who had proven little other than their ability to talk ambitiously about the potential of the Internet. Firms that went public to great acclaim were bankrupt before the year was out, established companies opened their wallets to the tune of billions for acquisitions that in many cases proved worthless, and individual companies burned through hundreds of millions of venture funding before going out of business. Entrepreneurs, investors and cheerleaders chased the money without taking time to examine the means.

Time after time, the shareholder imperative has driven companies to extreme measures that deliver results in the short term but lead to implosion in the end. The tyranny of the share price means too many decisions are made with no criteria in mind except what is good for the next quarter's results. It is a mindset that, at the extreme, leads to corporate catastrophes like Carillion, the outsourcing company that went into administration in January 2018 with more than 43,000 employees on its payroll. In 2016 it had recorded revenues of £4.2bn and operating profit of £147m, paying out a record dividend to shareholders. Yet a series of delayed projects, spiralling debts and market desertion saw the company go under with just £29m in cash, against liabilities of over £7bn. A parliamentary inquiry into the collapse identified a 'rotten corporate culture', described how 'accounts were systematically manipulated to make optimistic assessments of revenue', and how the lead auditor KPMG was 'complicit' in 'complacently signing off the directors' increasingly fantastical figures'. Its report concluded that, 'The individuals who failed in their responsibilities, in running Carillion and in challenging, advising or regulating it, were often acting entirely in line with their personal incentives.' In other words, the system may not have made them do it, but it certainly didn't stop them.

As the case of Carillion shows, the shareholder-centric system can easily be something that leads companies into financially disastrous decisions and strategies, with major consequences for investors, employees, suppliers and customers alike. However, it goes further than that: we also need to acknowledge how it can encourage bad behaviour in business, a win-at-all-costs mentality that can erode morals and distort perspective. How else does a bank like RBS end up producing an internal memo where a manager in its notorious Global Restructuring Group gave advice under the theme of 'Just Hit Budget', including 'rope: sometimes you need to let customers hang themselves'?

As an investor I have seen exactly this sort of distorted thinking at first hand. The phrase 'it doesn't matter, you can't monetise the dead' is not what you expect to hear in a pitch meeting, but it was how one entrepreneur responded to my question about how his business would manage the personal information of customers after they had passed away. Everything this guy said was basically that as long as he could make a lot of money, he didn't really care about what customers did or didn't know about how their data could be used, during their life or after it. In his view, as long as something buried deep in the terms and conditions covered his back legally, it was fair game.

A stark example perhaps, but it brought home to me that there is still a school of business that follows directly from Friedman: as long as you're not breaking any laws, then you can do what you like as long as it helps to maximise profits.

The problem is where the logical extension of that conclusion takes you, which is the idea that anything goes, as long as the legal system doesn't stop you, customers or investors don't abandon you, and regulators don't clamp down on you. It's effectively daring some part of the ecosystem that a business relies upon to draw the line and stop it. The shareholder imperative can mean companies push the bounds of what is acceptable, and more, if there's enough money in it. At its worst, and I should emphasise that this far from universally the case, it enshrines bad business and questionable practices.

I don't come from the starting point that businesses and CEOs are going out into the world to do bad things. There are many companies that are responsible, deeply committed to the interests of their customers and employees, and who go out of their way to maximise their social impact. Moreover, at its best, business has the ability to be a force for good, driving change that improves people's lives and addressing challenges in society that governments are poorly equipped to tackle alone. But the important role that business has should not deter us from calling out the problems that exist in the prevailing model of doing business. In fact, if capitalism is to fulfil its positive potential, it is essential to do just that. It is not enough to plead simply that the worst offenders are outliers, the 'few bad apples' in an otherwise blameless bunch. This misunderstands both the idiom and the problems inherent in the status-quo model of business. Because the problem with bad apples is that they do not rot alone; they spoil the entire barrel. In the same way, the problems of the shareholder-centric system are not contained within its most high-profile failures. The short-term mindset it enshrines, where immediate problems can overshadow more structurally important ones, is an issue for every business where shareholders hold too much sway. That means the various problems described so far are not occasional aberrations but intrinsic to the model: a feature and not a bug.

Has this not always been the case? Have companies not been ruthlessly prioritising their immediate financial interests to outrun the competition since cavemen were trading in flint? It is tempting to think so, but not all evidence bears out the assumption. A compelling counterpoint comes from Arie de Geus, a former Shell executive who led a research exercise for the oil giant in the 1980s, looking at the principles supporting some of the world's oldest and most successful companies. These ranged from chemicals conglomerate DuPont, founded in 1802, to the Swedish manufacturer Stora, whose original charter dates to the 14th century. He summarised his findings in a 1997 article for the *Harvard Business Review*, drawing out the characteristics of what he defined as 'living companies', with the capacity to sustain and renew themselves consistently across generations. De Geus drew a stark contrast between companies that were organised around owners, and those who prioritised all of their people.

Companies who focused on their shareholders were 'like a puddle of rainwater', he wrote: capable of growing but not moving, a fundamentally static entity that struggles to adapt to changing circumstances. 'Puddles of water cannot survive much heat. When the sun comes out and the temperature rises, the puddle starts evaporating.'

By contrast, he defined the companies that had lasted across centuries as 'river companies', constantly changing but also more permanent, focused on the continuity of the whole and not the stability of individual components. 'The living company is a river company,' he concluded. 'In such an organisation, managers regard the optimisation of capital as no more than a necessary complement to the optimisation of people. To build a company that is profitable and will live long, managers take care to create a community. Processes are in place to define membership, establish common values, recruit people, develop employees, assess individual potential, live up to a human contract, and establish policies for graceful exits from the company.'

This analysis is helpful in highlighting the conflict at the heart of the shareholder model. Because if your overwhelming focus is delivering for investors, that can inhibit your ability to do good things for your consumers, employees and the wider community of which you are a part. It limits choice and flexibility, forcing companies to put the needs of one part over those of the whole. And by doing so, you can never hope to reach the most balanced and effective business decisions, especially for the long term. De Geus is clear about the nature of this choice: 'Many shareholders and senior managers are not interested in building a self-perpetuating work community. They prefer the company to remain a moneymaking machine for the benefit of an inner circle. Theirs is a perfectly legitimate choice, but those who make that choice must realise that there is no free lunch.'

The situation we find ourselves in has arisen because too many companies deny the reality of this choice. They assume that value created for shareholders is a necessary good from which all other benefit, to all other relevant parties, will flow. This belief has been the foundation for an economic system that enshrines too much inequality, encourages too much corporate malpractice and ultimately fails to drive the stable, sustainable economic growth that society depends upon. It is a system that gives insufficient credit to the power of capitalism to drive innovation, create prosperity and tackle socio-economic problems.

★★★

So what can we do about it? This is not about making an enemy out of shareholders. You can be a good, long-term-minded and deeply moral business while retaining a strong focus on your shareholders. In fact you have to maintain that focus because unless your business is economically successful, and delivering value to its shareholders as a result, it is not going to succeed in any of its aims. It is not the idea of shareholder value itself that is problematic, but the lengths to which it has been pursued, and the system that has resulted that often cannot see past the shareholder to the other needs and responsibilities a company has.

Shareholders deserve to enjoy the successes and wear the failures of a business as much as any other constituent; they do not deserve to have their position shored up by decisions that are more in their individual interest than that of the company as a whole. The shareholder value system has contributed to business losing its perspective about what and who matters. For a reboot to become possible, that perspective first needs to be regained.

CHAPTER 2

UNDER PRESSURE

The status-quo system, one which prioritises share-holders above all others, presents one of the most compelling reasons for why a reboot in business is required: moving beyond the over-emphasis on investors alone to create a model that serves employees, consumers, society and the environment equally well, and which can over time combat the inequalities of the current system.

However, it is one thing saying that such change is required. Given we are talking about a system with roots stretching back almost 50 years, is it actually feasible? If the shareholder imperative can survive the dotcom boom and the cataclysm of the financial crash, why should we expect anything to change now?

The short answer is that technology is radically altering the business landscape, in different ways and from various directions, to the point where a reckoning with the status quo will be difficult if not impossible to avoid. In particular, new tools, platforms and relationships arising from technological change pose three distinct challenges to business, all of which directly threaten the ascendancy of the shareholder-centric model, and open the door to a new one.

The first challenge comes in the form of an onslaught of new technological possibilities, forcing businesses to sort the genuinely significant developments from the red herrings, and work out how they can adapt their business models accordingly in search of greater productivity and in the face of emerging competition. Technology is creating not just uncertainty for most businesses, but a series of decisions about what opportunities they pursue, how to balance technology with people, and how to bridge between their existing business model and the one that will be required in the future.

The second challenge is in how trust in business is being eroded as technology creates much greater transparency and encourages sharper scrutiny. This is partly a product of how customer relationships are changing, with digital platforms enabling consumers to become activists, whether that is raising attention to the perceived faults of a business, or encouraging people to take action against them. More than that, as customer records become digital and personal information is held online, there is a dawning debate over personal data: how much companies are collecting, how safely they are looking after it, and what they are using it for. Who controls personal information and where it travels are important questions that are only just starting to be seriously discussed at a mainstream level, not least in the context of the GDPR regulations.

It all adds up to a situation where companies are much more closely scrutinised, by consumers with digital platforms and organising capacity, motivated by fears about their personal data and privacy and in many cases carrying new expectations of the moral and social obligations of business. The great victim of this change becomes public and political trust in business. When you add in the increasingly high-profile controversies over high executive pay, corporate culture and sexism, the gender pay gap and some companies' questionable degree of willingness to meet their full tax burden, it becomes easy to see how an environment of enhanced scrutiny could quickly lead to a crisis of trust in business, and an undermining of the current model.

Thirdly, there is the challenge of how technology is changing work, and whether or not this is for the better. While technology should in theory be helping people to work more efficiently and sparingly, there is a tendency for smartphone connectivity to mean they actually put in more hours. The evidence suggests that people are broadly disengaged from their jobs, at the same time as becoming more stressed by them. In parallel, the dramatic dislocation that artificial intelligence is going to bring to many business sectors is something that is creating fears about how many jobs will exist in the future.

From the operational decisions companies are faced with, to the public perception of business, and the changing nature of the employment it supports, technology is driving instability for businesses on a number of different levels. In all three areas there are opportunities for business to do better – improving its results, reputation and the experience of employees – but equally there are significant risk factors in play. There is potential for a better model of business to emerge, but there is also scope for the current model to be accelerated, and for the power of technology to exacerbate the inequalities it has already created.

In either case, these challenges will bring into sharp focus the choices that every business has, and they are already making obvious the consequences of an approach that puts shareholders above all others, rather than as one important constituent among several. With consumers restive and employees both disengaged in the present and fearful about the future, the ground is shrinking beneath the feet of businesses who put the needs of these two groups below those of shareholders.

It is not just because the current model is broken that a reboot in how companies think, organise and act is required. It is because of the new challenges that new technologies are bringing, the instability they are creating and the decisions they will soon make necessary. I now want to explore each of these three challenges in more detail, before looking at the questions that arise for every business as a result.

Challenge 1: Technology isn't delivering

When I started my career in technology companies, during the dotcom boom, everything seemed and felt possible. It genuinely felt like we were on the cusp of transforming how business would operate, and that the emergence of a new networked world would open up a boom in business performance and potential. It seemed obvious that technology would be the enabler of more productive and successful enterprises, allowing businesses to work more efficiently and scale more rapidly.

Yet while there are undoubtedly pockets of progress – and a lot has changed in practice – the top-line picture is that the promised productivity boom isn't happening. According to the US Bureau of Labor Statistics, the years 2007–16 saw one of the slowest periods in productivity growth in business (excluding agriculture) on record. Productivity increased on average by just 1.1 per cent annually, compared to 2.7 per cent between 2001 and 2007 and an average of 2.3 per cent since 1947. Even if you accept the financial crisis will have had a significant bearing on those figures, it's clear that we are not seeing the technology dividend across the board that most, with good reason, predicted. According to the Bank of England, approximately one third of the UK's business population has seen no increase whatsoever in productivity since the turn of the century. Its chief economist, Andy Haldane, has said that 'most companies have below-average levels of productivity and a large fraction of them have seen no productivity improvement for several decades.' The Nobel laureate Robert Solow's 1987 observation, that 'you can see the computer age everywhere but in the productivity statistics', still seems as prescient as ever.

There are many things people and companies can do that were neither possible nor thinkable even a decade ago. But all that change hasn't added up to a significant improvement in either business productivity or overall economic performance, at least in developed countries (emerging markets, where smartphones are helping hundreds of millions access services for the first time, are a very different story). If anything, we have seen less benefit from technology over time, since the initial adoption of email and Internet technologies helped fuel the boom of the mid to late 1990s. According to a 2015 OECD report: 'From 2004, the benefits from the ICT revolution began to wane (in the US) and labour productivity growth in the most recent period has been the weakest on record in most OECD countries since 1950.'

If companies are already failing to make the most of available tools, the problem could be about to become more acute as a new generation of technology emerges and becomes commonly available. In theory, there is almost boundless potential for business in these innovations. Artificial intelligence could transform the efficiency of most companies, eliminating back office bureaucracy; quantum computing will blow away our current ideas of what processing power looks like; 3D printing has the potential to open up a new wave of hardware development as prototyping costs and time frames plummet.

All this is possible, but it will only become practical if business gets better at working with technology, and makes more effective use of the tools that emerge in the next decade than it has done with those of the previous two.

That is easier said than done. Many established companies are running on legacy systems that are costly to maintain, limit flexibility in product development and tend to perform worse and worse over time. With one hand tied behind their backs, they then have to operate in a landscape where hype around technology is nonstop, over-claiming is rife, and there is little in the way of clarity about when and how disruptive technologies are going to become usable and profitable business tools. The challenge is in trying to carve out a clear path of progress for your business amid this widespread confusion.

It is not just technical considerations here that matter, but timing. Whatever bold predictions are being made about this tool or that, what actually matters are the realities of how they will integrate with your business and its needs. To be worthwhile, technology has to be something that your team can make good use of, and which in turn delivers tangible benefit to both your customers and business performance. It's all too easy to end up implementing something that employees will bypass, customers won't be interested in, and which ends up costing more than it saves. Invest too early, when either the technology or the people who need to work with it aren't ready, and that will likely be your fate. Wait too long, and competitors will have surged ahead of you.

These are delicate, long-term decisions that often do not sit easily alongside the unremitting demands of shareholders for their next dividend. I know from experience that investors will often insist that technological development either be postponed, or carried out too quickly, because its being done at the right time, and taking as long as it needs, often doesn't satisfy their need for certainty. As technology becomes an even more significant component of commercial success than it already is, companies need to make better decisions about how to use and work with it. Achieving that will almost certainly mean loosening the shareholder straitjacket, and making decisions that might not serve this year's bottom line, but which will nevertheless pay dividends over time.

Transformative technologies are going to be the defining factors in the business landscape of the next decade, but it is how they are implemented in practice rather than the promise they hold in theory that matters. The bottom line is that many businesses have so far struggled to realise the full benefits of Internet-era technologies, even as they have implemented and integrated them. Unless a better approach to working with and organising around technology becomes widespread, that problem is only going to get worse as the trickle of new technologies becomes a flood.

Challenge 2: Trust has been eroded

As companies struggle with the challenge of integrating new technology, they are also facing a new reality where tech platforms are fundamentally altering their external relationships and reputation. If the decline of trust in business has been a long-term trend (the proportion 'very dissatisfied' with the size and influence of major corporations has risen from 17% in 2001 to 36% in 2018, according to Gallup), it has appeared to accelerate in recent years. In an increasingly volatile environment, some of the world's most prominent companies have been left scrambling to limit severe damage to their public image.

The crosshairs have narrowed particularly dramatically on technology companies. Brands that until quite recently were widely hailed as the heroes of the new digital age – from Facebook to Uber and Amazon – now find themselves vilified as the reinventors of an extractive, anti-competitive form of capitalism that harks back to the robber barons of the late 19th and early 20th centuries.

These platforms, which provide so many of the services that underpin our on-demand economy, are coming to attract nearly as much opprobrium for their failings as they did praise for their progress in easier times. Companies that made their name by promising the future have become mired in the problems of the present: accused of everything from facilitating the spread of misinformation and extreme content, to undermining the fabric of communities and even democracies, flouting regulatory frameworks and tax codes, and showing disdain for customer data and employee welfare alike.

This criticism has ranged from Uber, justly pilloried for revelations about its workplace culture, its use of software to evade authorities, the treatment of its drivers and a gung-ho attitude to regulators; to Amazon, notorious for its tax management and treatment of warehouse workers; Facebook, charged with undermining everything from child safety to the integrity of democratic elections; and Apple, criticised for its pricing of new products and attempts to render old ones obsolete.

Emerging out of the shadow of the global financial crash, technology companies were meant to be a break from the past, to represent a new model, suffused by the democratic, all-empowering and liberating power of the Internet. It was meant to be about a better way, leaving behind the worst elements of the old corporate pastiche, and opening the doors of power, wealth and influence to the majority. And yet these companies now find themselves portrayed as monopolisers, tax avoiders, regulation-busters and data hoarders: the worst of the old capitalist excesses, on a new scale made possible by technology. The same, but if anything even worse.

If the recent travails of big tech partly reflect a growing realisation of the implications of its model – from how it uses customer data to how its platforms are encouraging abuse and fake news, and the damaging role of all-pervasive technology in our lives – they also stem from the greater expectations that all parties now hold of the companies they buy from, work for and invest in.

The people on whom companies depend have choices: they can shop elsewhere, switch services, or move jobs with greater ease than ever before. The balance of power has shifted from provider to consumer in almost every sense; which means companies are having to compete harder than ever for customer, employee and investor loyalty.

So the idea that employees will always sell themselves to the highest bidder, and consumers flock to the cheapest seller, simply no longer holds water. It is no longer enough to be the best, or the best value. Good intentions, and positive impact, are rising up the scale of what people expect from the companies they work for, do business with, buy from and invest in. For example, it's estimated that 85 per cent of millennials (those born between the early 1980s and the mid-1990s) make recommendations and purchasing decisions based on the social good a company achieves. If good behaviour is being rewarded, then the bad is being punished in equal measure. High-profile brands increasingly face social media-orchestrated boycotts, from the #DeleteUber movement, which saw an estimated 200,000 users delete their accounts after the firm was perceived to have broken a taxi strike in protest at the Trump administration's immigration policies, to the swathes of Facebook users who quit the platform after the Cambridge Analytica data breach was revealed in March 2018.

Investors too are raising their standards. Larry Fink, CEO of the world's largest asset manager BlackRock, has said the following to companies it invests in: 'Society is demanding that companies, both public and private, serve a social purpose. To prosper over time, every company must not only deliver financial performance, but show how it makes a positive contribution to society.'

As trust declines, consumers are behaving in more volatile ways, demanding more and responding more decisively when their expectations are not met. The same atmosphere of distrust extends to politicians and regulators, those with much wider-ranging powers of sanction. A criticism of the corporate status quo was a central plank of the Trump campaign for President, whose concluding advert spoke of the 'global power structure that is responsible for the economic decisions that have robbed our working class, stripped our country of its wealth and put that money into the pockets of a handful of large corporations'. That language was mirrored by Jeremy Corbyn during the 2017 UK General Election, who launched his campaign by decrying 'yesterday's rules, set by failed political and corporate elites we should be consigning to the past. It is these rules that have allowed a cosy cartel to rig the system in favour of a few powerful and wealthy individuals and corporations.'

Where politicians have spoken, regulators have acted, with the EU – led by its competition commissioner Margrethe Vestager – imposing a record $2.7bn fine on Google in 2017 for manipulating search results, and demanding that Amazon pay $250m over previous tax benefits later ruled illegal. It is now common to hear talk of how the big tech companies should be broken up as monopolies in the same way the oil giants of the late 19th century were.

This less permissive, more scrutinised environment means companies who focus on profit and legality to the exclusion of all other considerations are playing a dangerous game. They are gambling that their usefulness will outstrip behaviour that is becoming questionable in the eyes of employees, customers, investors and regulators. Companies can easily forget that their existence relies on a complex web of permissions to survive: from people wanting to work for you, to customers wanting to buy from you, investors wanting to back you and regulators permitting you a licence to operate.

People are no longer willing to look the other way. And while technology companies and data privacy might be on the frontline, this is a challenge that extends across the full business spectrum. Gambling companies are now being asked to account for the harm their products, especially high-stakes betting machines, cause to vulnerable people; FMCG companies are being regulated over the amounts of salt and sugar in their food; supermarkets challenged to reduce the volume of plastic waste they produce; and transport companies and utilities mandated to more clearly publicise their best-value tariffs. Tobacco companies in the US have been ordered by the courts to run television advertising campaigns on the dangers of smoking. While the gender pay gap is finally being made into a frontline business issue, with the UK government having ordered every business with more than 250 employees to report the equality or otherwise of its pay structure.

The message to business could not be clearer: companies that put the financial interests of their shareholders above the privacy or health of their consumers, who fail to pay their taxes properly or their workers equally, and who don't act to limit damage to the environment, are going to have change forced upon them, whether that is by government intervention or consumer activism. Business can no longer get by through simply offsetting wrongdoing and addressing only its most blatant shortcomings. Instead it must create a better model, one that actively embraces these new expectations and responsibilities, and which over time can win back the trust of consumers, employees, investors, regulators and politicians alike.

Challenge 3: Work isn't working

As the reach of technology in business grows and grows, it is not just creating commercial confusion and stoking an atmosphere of distrust. It's also having a clearly detrimental effect on many people's experience of work.

A 2013 Gallup survey of the global workforce, polling more than 225,000 workers across 142 countries, found that just 13 per cent felt engaged with their work. While a Harvard Business School study from the same year found half of the 12,000 white-collar workers in its sample felt their work lacked 'meaning and significance'.

Many feel increasingly alienated from their work, at the same time finding themselves doing more of it. While the long-term trend is for people to work fewer hours (according to the OECD, UK workers did 13 per cent fewer hours on average in 2016 than in 1970; and workers across OECD member countries, 11 per cent fewer), the short-term perception is that working hours are on the increase. An EY global survey of almost 10,000 managers found that 39% reported their working week had grown longer in the previous five years. A 2016 survey of UK workers by the Smith Institute think tank found that two thirds thought they worked longer than two years previously. Perhaps the long-term trend is being reversed, or maybe people's perceptions are out of whack with the reality. But the fact is that a growing number of professionals feel they are having to work harder now than they did only a few years ago.

Is more being achieved as a result? Not if you believe the Smith Institute respondents, only 10 per cent of whom said they felt more productive as a result of their longer hours. Despite the resilience (and elongation) of the eight-hour work day, most estimates suggest that people work effectively for less than half of that time. A 2016 survey of UK workers showed that people believe themselves to be productive for an average of only 2 hours and 53 minutes.

So we are (likely) working longer, probably achieving no more for it and almost certainly deriving less satisfaction from it. Technology that was meant to free us from work has actually led to us being more attached to our jobs than ever. An estimated 50 per cent of workers now check their work emails in bed, compared to 2002, when fewer than 10 per cent did so at all outside the office. It's not just that we can't switch off from work; there's also far more of it being created. Consider that, according to the management consultancy Bain & Co, the number of external communications the average executive receives in a year has grown from 9,000 in the 1990s to more than 30,000 today. Its study also suggested that an estimated 15 per cent of any company's collective time is spent having meetings, a figure that has risen every year since 2008.

The umbilical cord that technology has created between most people and their jobs may be contributing to increased levels of work-related stress. The British Social Attitudes Survey found in 2015 that 37 per cent of people found their work stressful, compared to 28 per cent in 1989. Government statistics show there were over half a million people in the UK in 2016–17 suffering with 'work-related stress, depression or anxiety', leading to 12.5 million lost working days. Workload was identified by 44 per cent as the cause.

How did we get to this point? It's certainly not the working world that technology was supposed to create, or one that those of us who have been around for a while expected it would. I remember when I got my first Blackberry, at a point in my career when I was doing endless business travel. How great this was going to be, I thought. My emails would be done on the go, I'd no longer arrive home tired to an overflowing inbox, and I'd finally have the time to learn Spanish. *Que no sucedió.* Instead of finally learning to tell my *empanadas* from my *fabada*, I discovered the timeless lesson that getting your work done promptly just means more will be created.

Rather than seeking to fundamentally reboot work to maximise the benefits of new technology, we have created a curious hybrid between the old world and the new one, where we have the tools and technology to change, but remain largely wedded to the fixed-location, fixed-hours model. A system that was designed to maximise productivity in the factories of the Industrial Revolution era still staggers on in the offices of today, table football and giant slides or not. And the evidence suggests people are increasingly unhappy, disengaged and unhealthy as a result. As the University of Manchester's Professor Tony Dundon has written, 'Technology may uplift some skills, but it also contributes to employment precariousness, with a culture of long and unsocial hours, where labour can be considered a cheaper alternative to techno-logical investments by firms.'

Rebooting business, therefore, must also mean rebooting our ideas about how and where work should be done, and what its purpose should be. An unhappy, disengaged workforce is also going to be an unproductive one. For a better model of business to be possible, we need to think more about how human needs can be met and talents unleashed in a world increasingly dominated by technology. Because ultimately, what is good for a company's workforce will also be good for its performance and productivity. No amount of technological change and disruption is going to alter that basic truth.

The key issues

Having spent so long putting the needs of shareholders first, business now faces a moment in time where the needs of all other stakeholders are coming to the fore and demand attention as well. Consumers are expecting more from the brands they buy from and advocate for, while being generally less trusting. Employees are increasingly dissatisfied with a model of work that is more burdensome than it needs to be. Politicians and regulators, who help determine companies' licence to operate, are becoming less permissive and more inclined to act.

The status-quo model of business is neither achieving the improved levels of performance and productivity that technology should have created, nor inspiring the trust, or supporting the kind of engaged and fulfilled workforce, that companies need to succeed sustainably.

A reboot is required, not just because there are obvious flaws in the existing model, but because there is so much untapped potential in business, from contributing more decisively to economic productivity and growth – both stubbornly sluggish since the financial crisis – to helping tackle social and environmental issues. Business is uniquely placed to start coming up with new and better answers about how we can live and work more happily in a fast-changing, increasingly technological world. Most of us spend most of our lives working for some kind of business. It is business where many of the innovations that will define our future are being pioneered. And it is business, compared to government, that has the agility to make rapid progress in helping address the challenges we face.

To achieve a reboot we need to re-examine all aspects of how companies think and operate: from internal processes and priorities, to relationships with customers and the outside world, the responsibilities they take on, and the environment that they create for employees. To explore how this can be done, I want to break down the overall question of how we reboot the broken model of business into three more specific ones that arise from the challenges I have outlined:

1. How can companies organise for and achieve change?
2. How does business win back trust?
3. How can companies create stable, meaningful employment in a more technological future?

The first question addresses how businesses can respond to the confusing landscape of emerging technology and changing customer needs, and make better use of the former to satisfy the latter. The second looks at what company leaders can do to inspire greater trust, within their teams and among the wider public. And the third is a question of how companies get the most out of their people as business becomes more technologically driven, while in turn addressing the crisis of engagement and meaning that is becoming clear in today's labour market.

In this chapter I have focused on challenges, but it is important to remember that everything discussed here also represents an opportunity for every business: to become more productive and profitable, more respected and better supported, and to create thriving teams of people who are interested in and committed to their work.

Technological change is forcing decisions about the kinds of businesses we want to build, the jobs we want to have, and the working world we want to carry forward into an era in which machines will play a much greater role. These are choices, and leaders in business have free will about the kind of economy and society they want to help shape. There is no burning building into which the world's founders and CEOs are somehow locked that necessitates prioritising machines above humans and demands that the needs of shareholders always come first.

We have these choices, and we need to exercise them. There is a possible future where shareholder capitalism is hitched to the wagon of increased machine power, accelerating the inequalities and concentration of wealth that we are already starting to see. And, with many more versions in between, there is an opposite future where companies choose to meet their obligations to society as a whole, attract customers, employees and investors who are aligned with their values, and show that it is possible to be hugely profitable while also enriching people's lives and being a significant net contributor to the good of society. That doesn't seem like pie in the sky. It feels like a good option, something that is achievable but above all, desirable.

PART II

Rebooting business

'It is capitalism that opened the gates to the Land of Plenty, but capitalism alone cannot sustain it.'

Rutger Bregman,
Utopia for Realists:
And How We Can Get There

CHAPTER 3

THE QUESTION

Go into any boardroom in the world, ask these three questions and I challenge you to find a single person who will answer no to any of them.

Is technology fundamentally changing our industry? Yes. Do we need to reorganise our business to take advantage of this and avoid being left behind? Yes. Are we worried that more technologically enabled competitors (existing and emerging) are getting ready to steal our lunch? Yes.

The nodding and raising of hands is only going to stop when you ask a different question: What exactly should we do about that?

It is much easier to diagnose a systemic, wide-ranging problem – the turbulence that technology is creating for many incumbent business models – than it is to define a solution. And that is the challenge many businesses are now struggling with: devising a treatment plan for technological change that will provide a long-term cure without killing the business they already have.

There are plenty of things that most companies know and acknowledge about what a more techno-logical world means for them. Companies know, at the most basic level, they need to find new ways to reach and retain customers who live and do business online. They know that emerging technologies present opportunities, from automating business processes to understanding and anticipating their customers' needs better through big data, and devel-oping more technological products and services. They recognise that this will mean some changes, perhaps profound, to their existing business model and structures. And they realise that failing to act will almost certainly mean ceding ground to compet-itors, perhaps decisively.

Technology is becoming the defining obsession of companies across all sectors, which is why you will hear CEOs of automakers, utilities and even Big Tobacco talk about themselves as tech companies. It's no empty boast or aspiration. Car manufacturers know that there exists a not-so-distant future when they will no longer be able to sell petrol or diesel vehicles. Tobacco companies think that same future will be one in which they will no longer sell cigarettes. As a result, billions are being ploughed into the research and development of cleaner, tech-enabled alternatives. It's not just about companies with a health or environmental deficit, either. What about accountancy firms, as financial reporting and audit becomes automated? Insurance companies in a world where car ownership declines precipitously over time? Retailers if no one wants to go out shopping any more?

There are answers to all those questions: alternative business models, product models and service lines to be pursued. The problem is how you get from here to there. This is where the evidence suggests many are currently falling down. According to the market intelligence firm IDC, an estimated 70 per cent of corporate transformation projects will fail. Other surveys put the failure rate at similar or even higher levels. Businesses, especially large ones, freely admit that organisational failures are holding back their attempts to change. When Bain & Co partners Chris Zook and James Allen researched the growth hurdles facing established companies for their 2016 book, *The Founder's Mentality,* they found that almost every executive they polled (94 per cent in companies with revenues greater than $5bn) blamed 'internal dysfunction – not lack of opportunity or unmatchable competitor capabilities – [as] the main barrier to their continued profitable growth.' Problems they recorded included 'we've lost touch with customers', 'we're drowning in process and PowerPoint', and 'we have no shortage of opportunities, but somehow we can no longer act decisively'. The conclusion – that companies need to find better ways to organise in pursuit of change – seems clear.

So while the vast majority of companies accept the imperative to change in order to survive (only 8 per cent of those surveyed in a McKinsey study said their 'current business model would remain economically viable if their industry keeps digitising at its current course and speed'), not many seem to be making a particularly good job of it.

There are many reasons why this could be the case. Transformation projects can be unwieldy beasts, with goals that are too loosely defined, timetables that aren't tight enough to galvanise action, and a lack of leadership buy-in. Badly conceived or poorly managed change programmes will easily run into the weeds or become bypassed by people in a company who will carry on as they always have, following the path of least resistance.

These are some of the practical difficulties that companies trying to reboot themselves face. However, they are the symptoms and not the cause of the problem, which arises from a more fundamental mistake. Companies who accept the need for an overhaul of some sort are in many cases going on to ask themselves the wrong question. They reach for an idea that carries all the connotations of convention-busting, market-leading, reputation-defining brilliance. They ask, 'How do we innovate?'

The idea of innovation is a compelling lure. For many, it is synonymous with Silicon Valley. It's Steve Jobs and Elon Musk. Moon-shooting unicorns. Category-killing breakthroughs. It's the cool stuff that the kids in skinny black jeans are constantly disrupting, and the venture capitalists are funding halfway to space. It's something impossibly different and new that you just have to get your hands on. Blockchain, virtual reality, nanotechnology: we might not fully know what they are or what they can do for us, but we know we can't afford to miss out on them. Because someone somewhere is doing something with them that represents an existential threat. Minds wander and wallets open in the face of that fear alone.

Even as some tech reputations have been tarnished in the last year or two, many still look to Silicon Valley as the mountaintop of modern business, the example to be followed if you are ever going to succeed. It's why corporates are scrambling to make themselves more attractive to engineers who have done time at a Google or Apple; why you can hardly move in US business magazines for articles about when Valley CEOs get up in the morning; and why seemingly every new business you get pitched as an investor is presented as the Uber for this or the Facebook for that.

Silicon Valley has achieved many things, but perhaps one of its most pervasive legacies, especially within the business world, is how it has relentlessly marketed the concept of disruptive innovation. It has created the mirage that commercial success is about changing the category, overturning the market, and shocking the world. It has spread a compulsive fear of missing out among businesses that worry that they are going to get left behind or miss the next big thing. No matter that the Valley has produced many more duds than it has live unicorns (a study from Harvard Business School lecturer Shikhar Ghosh suggested 75 per cent of venture-backed Valley start-ups will fail to make back their original investment). It is the most powerful marketing machine in the corporate world and it has embedded its mythology firmly in the collective mindset. As a result, some start-ups seem to prioritise the achievement of unicorn (billion-dollar paper valuation) status as an end in its own right, rather than as the by-product of building a sustainable and successful business model.

There are two problems with this mindset, especially when you try and apply it to the majority of more traditional businesses, or those starting in established industries. The first is that becoming a company on the scale of Google or Amazon is not a realistic goal. And the second is that innovation, for many in business, is not a helpful objective or way of thinking.

If you go and ask 20 CEOs or heads of innovation what the word means, no two answers will be the same. Innovation has acquired so many definitions and layers of meaning that it can conceivably be used to justify anything from a simple plug-in to an entirely new product. Too often the idea of innovation – written into annual reports, enshrined in dedicated committees, and sprinkled like holy water onto job titles and descriptions – is more of a comfort blanket in the face of confusing change than a practical call to action.

There are some exceptions. If you are a business that is genuinely engaged in building the next iPhone, developing a pioneering medical treatment or trying to bring quantum computing or nanotechnology to market, then it's fair and right to talk in terms of innovation. But that is where the definition should start and end. The term innovation should be reserved for talking about those pioneering genuinely new market opportunities and creating things that do not yet exist, which will entail genuine scientific and technological expertise, and in most cases a hefty R&D budget.

The vast majority of companies cannot afford this, and are not actually trying to do it. They are in existing industries, delivering products or services that are well defined, and trying to find technological means to do that more efficiently, build the next generation of related products and services, and serve customers more effectively. I would define that not as innovation, but improvement. It is about delivering more and better for your customers, growing your business and outpacing your competitors. The objective here is not to rush out and invent the unknown future, but to build a bridge between the worlds of today and tomorrow, moving at a pace that won't alienate your customers or lose them altogether.

So rather than starting a process of change with a question like 'How do we innovate?', you should be posing some less ephemeral and more practical questions. How do we optimise, how do we enhance, how do we improve? In other words, how do we make this business (or if you're a start-up, this industry) actually work better? Better for the people who work in it; better for those who buy from it; and better for the world around it.

That was the question I asked myself when I
started as Simply Business CEO in 2010. It wasn't
simple aspiration. The company was failing, and
within my first six months we would come close to
not being able to make payroll. The business was in
a mess because it was trying to do too many different
things – not just business insurance, which is now
our sole focus, but also commercial mortgages and
invoice factoring, where you become a broker in
unpaid business invoices.

My objective was simple: I wanted us to become
the first properly tech-enabled insurance player in our
sector. The industry was lagging behind on adoption
of technology, especially compared to the e-commerce
world I had been involved in at lastminute.com and
match.com. When you spoke to insurance CEOs back
in 2010, they would talk about technology as an IT
problem and a cost line, not a tool that could radically enhance the service they offered to customers.
The challenge we set ourselves was to apply modern
methods to insurance, an industry which in its fundamentals hasn't really changed since the 17th century.
We've used technology to improve customer service,
and digital marketing, data science and machine
learning to build better customer insight, and we built
a new tech stack that allows us to develop and upgrade
products continuously, where the industry norm was
then once every few months.

We did a lot of things that made a big difference
to how our business operated, improved over time and
met the needs of customers. It wasn't revolutionary,

pioneering or even especially innovative compared to what was going on in other sectors. Still, it has helped us become the biggest UK company in our sector, to grow our customer base to almost half a million small businesses in the UK and a growing presence in the US, and be consistently ranked as one of the UK's fastest-growing technology companies.

A lot of that success has been down to the team we were able to recruit, the culture we created and the ethos of experimentation we instilled. However, I don't think any of that would have been possible unless we had started with the right question: not how to create the ideal business model, but how to improve and optimise the one we already had, and how to make that improvement continuous over time. If that sounds simple, I make no apology. The worst thing a business can do when facing a complex set of choices about how it responds to changing technologies, changing customer needs and a changing competitor set, is to make its own approach more convoluted than it needs to be. A simple question, which yields simple answers that you can set in motion, is infinitely more valuable than a bells-and-whistles innovation strategy that no one really knows what to do with. A lot of companies think they have failed at change because they didn't find the right answer; but it's just as likely they started off by setting themselves the wrong question, and framing the wrong objective.

Starting with the question of improvement rather than innovation doesn't just help you to focus on the challenge at hand and develop ideas and experiments you can put into practice. It can also help avoid two of the main pitfalls that lie ahead of any company looking to reboot its business model: a loss of focus on the customer, and bad timing of key structural or strategic changes. So before we go further and look at how companies should be working to answer the optimisation question, I first want to explore some of the things that you need to be obsessive about trying to avoid, and why asking a simple rather than a complex question can help you to do that.

Pitfall 1: Loss of focus on the customer

'The purpose of a business is to create and keep a customer,' the management theorist Peter Drucker once wrote. It's a philosophy that's hard to argue with; indeed so important are customers to any business that the idea of losing touch with them should be unthinkable. And, with an entire branch of the data science industry now dedicated to helping companies understand their customers in ever greater detail, it should be easier than ever to tailor products and services to what people want.

Yet despite that, one of the most pervasive causes of business stagnation or failure is the inability to properly understand the needs of customers, or even who those customers actually are (or should be). Consider Marks & Spencer, one of the UK's iconic retailers, which has now been struggling to turn around its clothing business – traditionally the cornerstone of the brand – for the best part of two decades. The reason? It can't really agree on who its customers are and what they want. The first UK retailer to record an annual profit of over £1bn in 1998, it had seen that figure plummet to £145m in 2001, with the clothing business particularly badly hit. Caught between trying to meet the needs of its traditional, older customer base and seeking to appeal to the changing tastes of a more fashionable market, it struggled to satisfy either the customers it already had or the ones it had ambitions to acquire. The confusion was perhaps summed up by a widely criticised and swiftly shelved advertising campaign: Exclusive for Everyone.

Should M&S be consolidating its base or trying to attract a new crowd? It's a question that has not really been answered in the years since, and by 2016 the clothing business was turning over just half of what it had in the mid-1990s. It led one shareholder, who had once designed clothes for the company, to declare at the 2015 AGM that 'Lord Sieff [former M&S chairman] must be turning in his grave. He used to say to me, "The day you lose your core customers is the day you lose your business", and he was right. Not only have you lost your core customers you have alienated them.'

It is at moments of change, exactly when you are trying to answer the question of how to make a business better and move with the times, that your customer relationships are most at risk. In trying to do new things, change old ones or reach new markets, companies risk the law of unintended consequences with those who are already loyal customers.

Another good example is McDonald's, which made significant changes to its offer in 2014, seeking to respond to the growing public interest in healthy eating and people's concerns over high levels of salt and fat in their diets. The company said it wanted to move from 'fast food' to 'good food served fast'. As a result, the calorie content of some classics was reduced, new healthier menu items were introduced, marketing was tilted to focus on healthier options and menu boards started to feature calorie counts. 'Hold the fries, pass the salad,' declared one *Reuters* news report. But what the fast food giant swiftly discovered was that its customers were giving it a pass altogether. An estimated 500 million customer visits were lost in the US in 2013–16, with internal research showing that consumers were defecting to direct peers such as Wendy's and Burger King and not to healthier or premium alternatives that had been considered the emerging competition. McDonald's had anticipated a customer who didn't really exist, and in the process lost a whole host of them who actually did. Sales only started to recover when a 'back to basics' approach was implemented, slimming down the menu and focusing on value. It had taken several years of slumping sales and the largest consumer-insight exercise in the company's history for McDonald's to conclude that what its customers wanted was bog-standard burgers sold cheaply.

What the McCautionary tale shows is how easy it is to lose sight of your customers when you are chasing change. In the rush to pursue a strategic goal of seemingly overwhelming importance – whether that is to respond to a technological opportunity or an assumed market need – companies can easily forget about the people who will ultimately be the difference between success and failure.

That is as true with enterprise customers as the mass market. A few years ago we were approached by one of the major global insurance brokers, who had decided they wanted a new online platform to better manage their network of independent brokers, and wanted us to build it for them. So in a couple of weeks we built a test version for them, and swiftly learned that such a platform wasn't needed or wanted: although there were efficiencies to be had for all parties through managing everything online, the brokers frankly didn't care about them. All that mattered to them was their commission. However convinced the brokerage company had been that this new online tool was what they needed, their customers didn't agree, and as such it would have been a mistake to proceed. It was only because we took an experimental approach to testing the idea that a project doomed to failure was nipped in the bud before it could run up too many costs.

A call to innovate can too easily become an inward-looking exercise, where a business looks to itself and not those who are actually going to buy goods and services. It means you grapple with an unseen, unknown enemy – what the future is going to bring and how to meet it in the middle – instead of bringing a laser focus to the challenge of what your customers are going to want and how you can do better for them. It encourages you to make assumptions in isolation from the customer and without sufficient empathy for their needs or perspective. At its worst, it becomes a sort of vanity contest in which you measure progress against your competitors rather than organising in the best interests of your customers. In the end, those customers aren't going to thank you simply for that fancy new innovation lab you just opened; but they will if their problem gets resolved in half the time.

All of which reinforces the importance of starting with the right questions, grounded in the realities of your existing business and customers, as you grapple with the challenge of a reboot. Because the moment you lose sight of your customers, your business is going to suffer no matter how perfectly scoped and executed your plan for change may be. So if you ever find yourself in a meeting asking the question of how to change, do better, or optimise your business model and realise that no one has mentioned (or better still, asked) the customer, then that is the moment to stop and try again.

Pitfall 2: Timing

The second pitfall to be aware of when preparing to reboot is timing. The why, how and who of making a significant change to your business model are all-important. But everything can still come apart if you get the 'when' wrong.

Business professors Charles O'Reilly and Michael Tushman addressed this tension in a 2004 paper on what they called the 'ambidextrous organisation'. Like Janus, the Roman god with eyes in the back of its head, they wrote, 'general managers and corporate executives [...] must constantly look backward, attending to the products and processes of the past, while also gazing forward, preparing for the innovation that will define the future.'

O'Reilly and Tushman were posing what remains one of the most pressing questions for any business: where should you draw the line between optimising what already works now, and pioneering what you think your business and its customers will need in the next 2, 5 and 10 years? How do you prepare for the future without compromising or even tra-ducing the business model that you already have? Or, as our parent company Travelers talks about it, how do you simultaneously perform and transform as busi-ness, without losing ground on either front?

An example that illustrates this well is one brought to my attention by Travelers CEO Alan Schnitzer: Ford. In the past two decades, the car maker has experienced a rollercoaster ride, rushing to adapt to a revolution in transport that spans the emergence of autonomous vehicles, new environ-mental standards and the changing ways in which people travel. Not only have these technological, environmental and cultural changes posed some fundamental challenges to the business model of one of the world's original mass manufacturers, it has also helped spawn some of this generation's most prominent technology companies, notably Uber and Tesla.

At different times in the last 20 years, Ford has been regarded both as a symbolic victim of change and as a poster child for corporate transformation. It has had two CEOs who met ignominious fates, and another who was regarded as an extraordinary success. Its experience has been salutary in demonstrating the challenges of achieving transformative change, and at the same time cautionary in what can go wrong when the pursuit of change cuts across everyday business needs.

Ford's scenic route to the future began in the late 1990s, under CEO Jacques Nasser. In 1999, *The Economist* wrote that he wanted 'to turn Ford from a boring old car maker whose shares achieve a price-earnings ratio of only ten, into a consumer products and services company commanding a multiple of more like 30.' That ambition was underpinned by a spree of esoteric acquisitions, including the repair shop chain Kwik Fit and a scrapyard business. More striking was his outlook on technology. In 2000, he unveiled a series of concept vehicles that now seem remarkably prescient, with a touchscreen dashboard featuring a range of what we would now call apps, a voice-activated system, and a focus on the vehicle as connecting rather than isolating its user. 'After little more than 100 years the car is no longer just a people-mover; it is the internet on wheels,' reported the *Guardian*.

Three years before Tesla was founded, eight years before the App Store opened, and over a decade before connected cars were a mainstream topic, Nasser's Ford had imagined the car of the future. In addition to the high-concept 24/7, he had poured investment into e-commerce and added an electric-vehicle company to his roster of acquisitions. An impressive-looking change programme, but in business terms it was a failure. Amid mounting losses, major product recalls and a slumping share price, Nasser was shown the door in 2001. His acquisitions were discarded and the focus returned to the 'nuts and bolts' that he had scorned as outdated.

That focused approach later yielded significant success under the leadership of his successor-but-one, Alan Mulally, who led Ford through the financial crisis as the only major American auto company not to need a government bailout. He arrived in 2006 at the bottom of a downward spiral, with a $12.6bn annual loss (the worst in the company's history) and assets including the company's logo mortgaged to raise funds. His subsequent turnaround, with a focus on a simplified product set, a unified culture and the core Ford brand, won widespread plaudits as one of the most successful in American corporate history.

Yet under the leadership of his successor, Mark Fields, attempts to put the company's foot down on change again stalled. The threat of self-driving cars, and the spectre of Uber and Tesla, led to another acquisitions binge, and an attempt to define Ford as a mobility rather than a car company fell flat. Supportive headlines in the technology press ('Meet the new Ford, a Silicon Valley software company') could not soothe investors' concerns over a strategy that was seen as incoherent, and insufficiently focused on the core. 'It is almost as if history has repeated itself,' a *Forbes* analyst wrote of the similarities between the Fields and Nasser eras. 'Ford acquired many new businesses in an effort to expand in a short amount of time while losing focus on the automotive operations.' The share price fell by 40 per cent, and Fields was out after three years.

Is there a lesson to be learned from Ford's experiences, other than to try and avoid sectors where Google and Tesla become your future competitors? I think there is, and it is about the pacing of change. However significant the speed of technological change appears to be, and however threatening emerging competitors seem, your essential compass point needs to be your own ecosystem: the customers, employees and investors on whose permission your success ultimately depends. If a company rushes ahead of its stakeholders, a loss of understanding can easily become a crisis of confidence, and a fast route to the exit door for the programme of change and its creator. Nasser and Fields focused too much on innovation in isolation, got their timing wrong, and were swallowed up as a result.

It is not enough for a CEO to have a compelling vision of the future and the strategy to build it, even if hindsight eventually proves them to have been right. You also have to pick your moment, one at which the business and its core constituents are ready to get behind the idea. That doesn't mean you have to travel at their pace or ignore pressing future concerns that no one else has yet fully considered; indeed you have to challenge your investors, stretch your team and tantalise your customers in order to succeed. But unless you time a programme of change for when your business is actually ready to bear it, you are almost certainly doomed to watch it fail.

★★★

When you are preparing to reboot your company, and are surveying the landscape of change, threats and opportunities that surrounds you, it can seem overwhelming. There is so much to take into account, from the technologies that could make a difference, through the changing needs of customers and the activity of competitors, to the challenges of making change happen within your organisation. You have to think about the means and mechanisms for change, the customer response you want to achieve, and how to pick the right moment to act. You need to have eyes everywhere and good instincts for the problems and unintended consequences that are bound to emerge.

Getting all that right, and making the right decisions at the right time in a way that doesn't harm your established model, inconvenience your customers, spook your investors, frustrate your team, or leave you scrabbling to keep up with competitors, can feel like an impossible balancing act, but that's the fun and challenge of running a business.

As I have suggested, it also points to one central need, which is to make things as simple as they can possibly be. Amid all this complexity, a plan for change that is itself complex is just asking for trouble. You need simple objectives, straightforward means, and a plan that can be easily communicated and understood across your organisation, whose results will be equally transparent to your customers and external audiences.

And that is why it is so important that your starting point should be a simple and tangible question – How do we make this business better? – not one that takes you into the jargon jungle of innovation. To focus on improvement instead of innovation is not about a lack of ambition or intent, but involves being more focused in how you organise your business in the face of uncertainty. It doesn't mean that you limit yourself to doing the same things you have always done, or rule out significant changes to your business model. Nor should there be any shame in having focused, realistic goals rather than towering aspirations. I'm a huge admirer of companies who want to reach for the stars, but that doesn't mean it needs to be the case for everyone. Plus, if everyone is planning next Friday's trip to Mars, who's going to take the bins out on Sunday evening?

By focusing on improvement in place of innovation, you help ensure that the changes you make, whether radical or incremental, are grounded in the needs of your customers, rooted in the realities of your business as it currently exists, and timed absolutely right. You can be extremely ambitious while keeping your ear to the ground, and being constantly on the lookout for hidden traps. You don't impede progress by taking these precautions; you actually help smooth its path.

CHAPTER 4

THE ANSWERS

Once you have set yourself the question of how to improve, how should you then go about seeking the answers?

The inbuilt business instinct at this point is to write a plan. A bells-and-whistles, forest-thinning, every-angles document that games out possible scenarios, weighs all possible evidence and reaches logical, data-drenched conclusions that dare anyone to gainsay them.

In theory plans are great things. They give confidence to your team and investors, they direct progress and they provide yardsticks against which to measure it.

But in an environment of constant change, traditional planning has fatal weaknesses. What looks good on the page often doesn't match up to a reality that is constantly shifting in terms of available technology, customer needs and short-term business problems. A prescriptive template and approach is not much use when nothing else you are dealing with is fixed or certain.

What you need is the flexibility and agility to change course, based on the evidence in front of you right now, not the strategy that was decided in committee six months ago. Just as the notion of innovation can turn a business inwards and make its focus intangible, a reliance on planning takes you away from the customer and the things you can do to help them right now.

Instead you should be thinking in terms of experimentation to find answers. In recent years, thinkers and entrepreneurs like Eric Ries have helped to popularise the idea of the lean organisation, where the agile approach widely used in software development is applied to company building as a whole. Ries argues that everything should be organised around the feedback loop of 'build-measure-learn': developing minimum viable products, testing them with customers and applying learnings to iterate and improve. In *The Lean Startup,* he writes: 'The fundamental activity of a startup is to turn ideas into products, measure how customers respond, and then learn whether to pivot or persevere. All successful startup processes should be geared to accelerate that feedback loop.' In *The Startup Way*, he has since written about how the same approach can be applied to good effect by large and established businesses.

This more experimental approach is exactly what is needed to navigate the change that every company now faces. Some of your ideas are going to work and others won't; some will work but not the way you thought they would. Some problems will need to be attacked from an entirely different angle than you had first anticipated. Building lean allows you to work through all those possibilities, and it avoids the nightmare scenario of investing everything in the theoretically perfect, exhaustively planned solution that falls on its face the moment you press go.

In my early days at Simply Business I learned some valuable lessons about how an experimental approach can save you from major errors when you are trying to reboot a business. As mentioned, I was trying to introduce a more tech-enabled approach, using the techniques I had learned from e-commerce in a new industry.

What I hadn't allowed for was the trust imperative. Selling insurance is fundamentally different from holidays and dating, because it goes directly to people's lives and livelihoods. It is not a casual flutter or an indulgence. With the small-business owners who are our customers, the right insurance can be what keeps the lights on when an unforeseen event strikes.

That need for trust means people don't necessarily want the quickest and most efficient service you can provide; they also want to kick the tyres, get a feel for who you are as a company, and satisfy themselves that you are credible culturally as well as financially and in terms of customer service.

In practice, that meant two of the changes I origi-nally planned to make proved to be duds. The first was a plan to make our customer service online only. I thought people wanted the most efficient service, and that we should automate what had traditionally been carried out over the telephone. However, what we found was that many really like a human voice on the phone and would much rather things stayed that way. Even though 100 per cent of our customers initially come to us through online channels, we have consistently found that around half of that base prefers to speak to us by phone than to communicate purely digitally. This has meant that, far from the automation of much of the call centre function I had originally envisaged, we have continued to invest heavily in people to provide the service.

One of my other bright ideas was that we should make it easier for people to submit the information we need to provide a quote. The form we had was a five-page questionnaire, cumbersome and time-consuming. And who likes having to fill those things out? Well, it turned out, our customers do! I would have bet all day long that people would prefer the speed and efficiency of the new system we trialled, which in some versions had as few as three questions (name, postcode and company turnover – the rest to be modelled on proxies). In fact the opposite was true. The customers we tried it with didn't like the new version because they didn't trust it. The whole thing felt too quick and easy, and they didn't believe it could be a real product or provide a robust quote. They were happier with something that took a lot more of their time, because it gave them reassurance that their situation was being properly understood and analysed. The answer for this may lie in what some psychologists have defined as the 'effort heuristic', by which we perceive something to be of greater worth relative to the effort that went into producing it (which can also explain why we value hand-made objects over machine-manufactured equivalents).

My fundamental bias towards digital solutions and efficiency meant I wasn't giving enough thought to the impression this would create in the mind of the customer. People are not robots, and their reactions to change are not always as transactional as you would first assume. Improving speed and lowering prices are important aims in any business, but quick can easily be perceived as rushed, and good value as cheap. Just as you would get suspicious in a restaurant if a hot meal was delivered within a minute or two of having ordered it, our customers were seeing more efficient approaches to service as a proxy for corner-cutting. I had started with the right instincts, but what the experiments showed was that we couldn't ram speed and efficiency down our customers' throats. That was our priority; theirs was to have a relationship they could trust. Those two things had to meet in the middle to help us improve, by doing what we knew to be progressive but in a style and at a pace that our customers would be comfortable with.

In other words, some of the ideas I brought into the business when I started proved to be entirely wrong. Things that seemed obvious to me in theory turned out to be irrelevant or unhelpful in the eyes of customers. The traditional approach would have been to pursue those ideas as canon, build the new systems and products, and then unleash them on unwitting and unwilling customers. It would have been both time-consuming and a grave mistake, leaving us scrambling to make changes and probably reverting to the old approach. Instead, by experimenting, we learned what customers didn't want and, over time, what they actually did. I learned the value of experimentation by having it proved to me that many of my starting assumptions were wrong. In other words, the best decision we ever took was that I as CEO should make fewer decisions; and that we let an approach of constant experimentation sort the wheat from the chaff of which ideas to pursue.

A test-and-learn approach, trying before you buy, is essential to help you get stuff right, but just as importantly, to prevent you from going badly wrong. What you don't do in business can be as important as what you do. Minimising the footprint of poor bets and mistaken hunches is as much a component of success as picking and pursuing good priorities.

By experimenting you also learn one of the most important business lessons: none of us is an entirely rational thinker or decision maker. We are all influenced by our experiences and the biases they have instilled in us. Experiments put these biases to the test, sorting the mistaken assumptions from the ideas that might actually work. They are essential to helping answer the questions of how to respond to changing technology, meet emerging customer needs and build a better and more flexible model of business.

Experimentation is about finding a better way of choosing priorities and making decisions, answering the question of how to change your business not through assumptions and biases, but guided by evidence and feedback. It doesn't matter if that approach leads you to try things that don't work. In fact, you should make it something of a point of pride that you cull more ideas than you build. The team behind Google's core search engine product tested more than 2,000 product ideas (actual features, not just fixes and optimisations) over the course of a year and ended up building fewer than 500 of them. You have to be ruthless about what is and isn't going to work, and that means kissing a lot of frogs to find your product princes. Many small failures help you to carve out a path towards eventual success. Experimentation allows you to gauge whether what you are hearing, reading and picking up in your market intelligence can actually be shaped into something meaningful, that will capture the interest of customers and investors alike. It means you test what you believe to be true against what customers and employees actually want, without having bet the farm on them agreeing with you about what that may be.

As such, one of the most important ways businesses can reboot their thinking and organisation is by replacing the traditional sequence of planning and execution with one of hypothesis and experimentation. Just as Bob Dylan once spoke of being 'constantly in a state of becoming', you should be seeking constant reinvention for your company. Never assume or seek to identify a fixed conclusion. Rather keep going, doing more of what you discover works and less of what doesn't. In the same way you wouldn't dive head first into a pool of uncertain depth, it makes little sense to charge headlong into a future that is unpredictable at best. Instead think about inching forward and feeling your way towards a probable path ahead. Tiptoeing into tomorrow may lack the thunder and lightning impact that some favour, but on the plus side you're much less likely to trip and fall on your face.

Experimental layers

Experimentation becomes the bridge between the products and services a business already delivers and the ones it will in the future. It shapes how you approach both near-term customer problems and far-off technological disruptions. In the incremental improvements you seek in the everyday, and also in the bigger picture change you are having to navigate in the medium to long term, experiments are an essential compass for making sense of a changing landscape. Whether you are considering how to deliver a marginal gain for a customer today, or how you might take advantage of an emerging technology on a two- to five-year horizon, experiments create a framework for setting the question, exploring the problem and iterating your way towards a solution.

By taking an experimental approach, you are gathering feedback and insight you can use before you would have even finished writing a plan under the traditional system. The only thing you really need to get started is a decent hypothesis, whether that is about something entirely new you want to try, a change to an existing product, or a potential improvement to your customer-service operation. A well-functioning business should be generating hypotheses like these on a constant basis, through customer problems or requests that you encounter, ideas that people come up with or borrow from elsewhere, and an awareness of new technologies that you might use to your advantage. To keep the ideas coming, you need to 'get in the flow' of what is happening around your business: spending time with the technologists who are doing the most exciting new work in your industry and beyond, to see how it might be relevant for your company; putting yourself in your customers' shoes to try and understand both what they want right now, and how those needs are changing; and challenging yourself with potential threats to your business model, asking how you could respond to them. You want to get as close to where change is happening at possible, in both available technology and the customer mindset, so you can think and hypothesise about how to best link the two together.

A hypothesis doesn't have to be an exhaustively researched proposition and a fully worked business case in its own right. Indeed the whole point of experimentation is to shortcut all of that, letting the idea stand or fall on its own merits as you test it with actual customers. The only criteria should be that there is a reasonable chance your hypothesis will deliver some form of improvement, and that it is something for which you can quickly develop a testing mechanism.

You should be aiming to develop and test as many hypotheses as you can, ones that focus on the immediate needs of your business as it stands as well as more long-distance priorities. There are three specific layers of experiment you should be seeking to pursue in parallel: experiments that are about customer needs right now, experiments that help you to understand the potential of emerging technologies, and experiments that allow you to game out longer-term disruptions and opportunities.

i) Customer experiments

So far, what I have talked about are essentially product and service experiments, where you work on tweaking existing platforms and trialling new solutions to achieve the goal of constant improvement. This is all about finding new and better ways to do what you already do, harnessing emerging technologies, and achieving incremental enhancements to the speed, efficiency and quality of service.

These experiments, focused on your core business and existing customers, are an essential part of how you stay relevant and maintain competitive advantage.

They are about avoiding complacency, adding value and most of all staying close to exactly what customers want, and how that is and isn't changing.

The fundamental mindset you need here is that your products and services are not fixed, but fluid entities that can and should be improved on a continuous basis. How that is done will emerge from a combination of internal ideas, customer feedback, competitor analysis and what you learn from what doesn't work. With an agile approach, if someone has a convincing idea you can build a pilot within a couple of days, and start getting evidence straightaway.

One of the early customer experiments we carried out at Simply Business under my leadership was on continuous cover, where we auto-renew policies rather than ending after a fixed term. This was the first attempt at a new product since my predecessors had tried and failed to create something bespoke for van insurance. That had been developed under the waterfall method, where a project is developed in linear and sequential fashion from initial scoping through to development, design and testing, with a return to the previous stage if and when problems are encountered. The van project had taken a year to develop, not all of the assumptions had worked out, and it had ended badly on a number of fronts.

The legacy was that people didn't want to take on big projects; they had become associated with problems, recriminations and failure. So we developed the continuous cover idea as a low-risk experiment:

auto-renewing a handful of our customers and then getting feedback from them. We made it look like the process was automated, though at that point it was actually being done manually (known as a 'Wizard of Oz' experiment). Within a couple of weeks, we had established that customers liked the idea, and created a checklist of the elements we could most usefully automate. Put another way, without developing any new technology or diverting too many resources, we had gone a long way towards developing what would become an important product enhancement. By working closely with customers, we had gathered evidence to inform how we could effectively scale the product and build it into our core business. Rather than assuming what people would want, building it and hoping for the best, we were de-risking the process by getting the feedback up front. That was particularly important in this case, because what we discovered – that people liked and appreciated the auto-renewal service – was at odds with what many expected would be the case. One hypothesis was that customers would be suspicious about having their policy roll over without having directly initiated a renewal. Instead we found that people preferred having the admin taken away, and having the reassurance that they would always be covered. Rather than endless debate within the business about the advantages and drawbacks of the policy, the experiment allowed us to test the competing assumptions against what customers actually wanted.

Most of all, we had done it quickly and easily, and without any significant up-front investment in building a system before we knew whether it would work or not. There is a tendency in business to try and jump straight to the end solution once you have identified a problem or assumed customer need. By taking an experimental approach, we were able to do the minimum number of things needed to gather sufficient data that informed us on real customer intentions, and showed us what we actually needed to build. It's what our CTO calls 'building the suit and not the machine': getting to the point where you feel you are confident you have solved the customer problem before you invest in developing technology to meet it. It's when you try and develop before you have gained this understanding that you run into costly and time-sapping problems.

We took a similar approach when expanding our business into the US, our most important growth market. Rather than sending out a launch team to start building a putative American arm from the ground up, we started with what Eric Ries terms the 'leap of faith' assumptions, where you take the riskiest elements of your proposition and seek to validate these before going any further. We undertook at least six months of testing from our London office, trialling consumer response to example digital advertising, and exploring the regulatory hurdles, before we put anyone on a plane or paid rent on an office. That meant, by the time we opened up in the US, we had a good idea of what the customer demand was and where we could find it, and had confidence that we could get a viable business started very quickly. This approach doesn't teach you everything, but it does give you the ideal launch pad from which to grow, whether into new products, geographies or customer markets. Don't make assumptions and then rush to build the system; instead start small with an experiment, learn as much as you can as quickly as you can about how customers are going to respond to your proposition, and then build based on that.

Experimentation is also essential in helping you understand how to make better use of technology to improve your products and services, and the customer experience. For example, in our attempts to bring a new edge to our customer service, we have started experimenting with technology that can analyse some-one's tone of voice on the phone, automating how we collect customer feedback. This has long been a problem for customer service teams, with difficulties in both getting any feedback at all (the success rate is lower than 10 per cent), and then judging whether people are actually saying what they think. However, through analysing voice harmonics and the cadence and pitch of conversations, there is technology which can predict whether a participant felt positive or negative about their experience with us.

We trialled this not by building a bespoke system of our own, but by matching up the capabilities of two different providers: our telephony system Twilio, and Soma Analytics, a machine-learning company focused on health and wellbeing (full disclosure: I am an investor in the latter). Twilio has the ability to record all of our voice data, while the Soma algorithm, which is principally designed to help companies monitor the wellbeing of their employees, performs the tone of voice analysis. We believe the prototype we have created can predict whether someone will be a promoter or detractor with an accuracy of 72 per cent, based on tone of voice alone. That is likely to improve as more data is collected and integrated into the system.

This was an experiment which arose from our desire to better understand our customers, improve the data that supports our propensity modelling (predicted behaviour of a customer), and ultimately enhance the probability of people becoming and remaining customers because they are getting the service they want. In a business like ours, those relationships are the absolute lifeblood, and it's one of the areas we are most focused on using technology to try and improve.

That might have meant us trying to build a proprietary algorithm, or even creating our own telephony system. But there is really no need to do that when there are so many tools and systems out there. The challenge then becomes how you can bring together third-party tools to match your specific needs. There may be no single service or provider who offers what you are looking for, but that doesn't mean you can't find a way of knitting several together, as we did in this case, made possible because Twilio worked with us to build the feature and integration with Soma.

By experimenting with available providers and tools, we were able to stitch together something that met our needs without having to invest in the lengthy and costly process of building something from scratch in-house.

Of course, experiments exist to disprove new ideas as much as to enable them. So even when you are almost certain that you have come up with something good, you need to put it to the test to make sure customers are going to agree.

Not long ago, I started getting interested in the idea of providing a service that could help link tradesmen, who represent around half our customers, with people who are looking for trusted contractors. With our data on risk profiles and claims history, we could provide an accreditation for tradesmen that would give people a credible database from which to commission work, and our own customers direct sales leads. Instinctively it felt like a perfect fit, something that could sit neatly alongside our core business and provide real added value to existing customers. So we gave it a go, I wrote a plan myself and the team built a test version. And, lo and behold, the feedback was terrible; it just turned out that people weren't interested in the service, and though we tried a few different versions, none of them got any traction. I might not have liked the outcome, but I still had to respect it. Because that is what the experimentation is for: to show when what you are convinced is a good idea is actually inappropriate either for the customer base is it aimed at, for your business, or for that moment in time. Or perhaps all of them.

It's the same principle when you are considering some whizzy new gadget that promises to transform your business into the land of milk and honey. When we'd opened our US office and were looking for ways to improve transatlantic communication, we trialled something called Beam, which describes itself as a telepresence robot, and basically amounts to a screen mounted on a Segway. The robot can drive itself around the office to someone's desk, giving the absent party a virtual presence in their counterpart's office. It was meant to help our teams work more effectively together but, as it turned out, having an almost silent robot zooming around the office was freaking people out, especially when it crept up behind them and said hello without warning. It didn't instil confidence either, when I tried the kit for the first time with one of our senior developers, and the first thing it did was shoot across the office at 20mph and crash straight into a meeting-room wall.

When it comes to trying new things, people tend to assume that inspiration is the hard part. But ideas are everywhere. It is the application that counts: turning your concept into something relevant that adds value for your customers or employees. And that is where experiments provide the acid test, separating the horses with some serious running in them from the white elephants in waiting. If you commit to never fully building something you haven't first tested with your customers and evolved based on their feedback, then you give yourself the best chance of filling your stable with winners.

ii) Technology experiments

The second layer of experimentation is to explore trends and technologies that don't yet play an important part in your business, but which soon could. From machine learning to virtual reality, geospatial imaging and blockchain, the business landscape is rich in emerging areas of technology that we are promised will transform everything in sight. It's just not always clear what exactly you can do with them or how they might apply to your business in the short or medium term.

I'll freely admit, when one of my developers first asked me what I knew about blockchain a few years ago, I didn't have a clue what it was, let alone how it might apply to our business. That was well before the more recent craze that saw the bitcoin market explode, but it's still easy to be spooked when people start talking about a new technology with potentially seismic consequences for your market, and you feel ill informed about what it is, let alone what it could mean.

My approach in such situations is twofold. First to walk before we can run – investing time in finding out about the technology before trying to formulate a view on what the opportunity might be. And second, to trust in the people who are closest to what's going on to provide the best guidance. That's not, in my view, the big consultancy firms publishing reports to try and drum up business, but our own developers.

It was one of our development team who had first started talking to me about blockchain in 2013. With our agreement, he then set up a blockchain discussion group which we hosted. More recently, he suggested we run a hackathon, getting some devs together to experiment with ideas for potential applications. All we would need to provide was some space, a prize and some beer and pizza. We did, and the guy who won the prize is now building a business out of his idea.

At the time of writing I still can't tell you what we plan to do about blockchain (not because it's some great secret; we just haven't got to that stage yet). But through almost no investment at all, apart from supporting one of our team to pursue an interest, and helping convene others of a similar mind, we have started to position ourselves to make progress. We've educated ourselves about a technology that is almost certainly going to prove significant for our industry, and we've got to know some of the people in our market who are at the cutting edge of developing new applications. We've got an advance view of the thinking and developed some relationships that should place us well to partner with emerging players in the future.

What we haven't done is invest in building any technology ourselves or try to launch any applications for our customers. At this stage, our experiment with blockchain hasn't gone beyond the inquiry stage.

But we are creating foundations that will hopefully serve us well as our perspective on its potential applications becomes clearer.

The question of when to try and turn a flashy new technology into an actual product or service is a tricky one. Go too soon and you risk creating a gimmick, or something that is more interesting than directly useful. Wait too long, and you can be left watching from the sidelines while others steal a march.

As ever, you need to let your customers be your guides. If you can create a link between an emerging technology and an existing customer problem, and there is something there you can build and test, then you should go right ahead. If you are a stage earlier than that, then don't panic. There is always going to be a good deal of froth and bluster around any high-profile new technology. Big pronouncements will be made and some big investments may follow, not all of which will succeed. Being the first mover far from guarantees that you will be among the first serious beneficiaries; and chucking money into something you don't yet fully understand, at least in the context of your business, is not the kind of experiment that I would recommend. A better investment is in building that understanding, surrounding yourself with people who are at the cutting edge of change. The closer you get to what is going on, the better chance you have of starting to work out how you might apply it.

So start small, do your due diligence, and do what you can to get close to the smart people who understand both the technology and its potential applications. Build your profile as a business that is interested in, and supportive of, developers in the space. Develop a position that means, when the relevance of a new technology starts to become clear, you are ahead of the pack, with the insight, contacts and credibility to take advantage.

iii) Thought experiments

Beyond the customer experiments that inform how your business works today, and the inquiries into new technologies that could become relevant in the medium term, there is a third layer of experimentation that can help you prepare for the further-off future.

While I believe most of your attention needs to be focused on the present and near term, there is still an important place for thought experiments that take you to a more distant horizon and help you to consider what your business, industry and customers might look like in one, two or even three decades, time. This won't necessarily draw conclusions that you can make practical use of right now, but it does help attune your business to future threats and opportunities, and trends or technologies you should be monitoring as a matter of course. Working through possible future scenarios, and considering what your company's place in those might be, is an important part of ensuring that you are not taken by surprise when things change.

For example in my industry, where cars represent approximately one third of the UK's £30bn personal insurance market, one of the most obvious of these threats is the rise of autonomous vehicles. Self-driving cars, and an associated decline in individual ownership, could significantly undermine the existing customer base of most major insurance companies. And insurance is far from alone in facing up to a future where whole pillars of its basic business model are going to come under serious, even existential, threat.

How do you prepare for something that might not fully come to pass for decades, and where the pace and scale of change is nearly impossible to predict? How early do you start preparing for the creation of alternative revenue streams? Too slow and you don't give yourself enough time to evolve and anticipate the scale of change. Too fast and you risk compromising a still-flourishing core business and haring off down blind alleys in search of any possible change in order to mitigate expected losses.

How to respond? You may not be able to predict the future, but you can take a position on it. It might be that there is no worthwhile product or technology experiment to undertake right now, but that shouldn't stop you from engaging in a thought experiment that will help you to consider a range of possible outcomes and future options, including the new opportunities that change is creating.

My advice is to start with the most radical version of that future and work backwards. In the case of self-driving cars and insurance, we have to assume that individual car ownership will die out, say somewhere in the next 20–40 years (even if our best guess is that the reality will be less extreme). We need to consider what the market would look like in a world where nobody owns their own car, and the self-driving alternatives are so safe that the manufacturers are willing to insure them.

What happens then? You've lost a huge piece of your market, so the question becomes what could replace it. That's going to depend on changing consumer habits and needs: driving may have disappeared, but people will still be doing things in their lives that carry risk and could require insuring. What might those be? Where is the risk in people's lives going to lie?

Or, from another angle, what could insurance companies be doing outside their core business that helps provide people with the safety and peace of mind that is the industry's fundamental purpose? That might be a shift into personal services: on-demand repairs or maintenance, for instance. A whole new set of problems that companies could easily adapt to help solve.

Again, it always comes back to the needs of the customer. What are the customers of the future going to need, want and be willing to pay for? A good thought experiment for business will think not just in terms of grand sweeps of technology, but also about what change will mean for the consumer of that era. It imagines how the same business will be able to serve the children and grandchildren of its current customers, in new and different ways. It develops hypotheses and assumptions around what future human needs and interests will be.

So much of our thinking about the future is focused on technology: how it is going to develop, the changes it is going to bring and the impact this will have on companies and society. What we do not pay enough attention to is the free will of people in that relationship with technology. By drawing straight lines from the tools of today to the ones that technology may create tomorrow, we ignore the critical question of how humans are going to interact and engage with those new realities. We risk making the same mistake I discussed at the beginning of this chapter, which is to overestimate people's willingness to seek the most efficient route possible, and underestimate their desire to hold on to things that are not included in technologists' predictions for the future.

Unless you are hanging your hat on a drone army taking over the world by 2050, you need to be thinking about organising your business around the needs of tomorrow's customers every bit as much as you do today's. Where product experiments can help a business get closer to understanding the needs of its existing customers, you also need thought experiments to start scoping out what your future customers will need and want.

It is not perfect, but between what you know about your customers now, what you can assume about how technology will evolve, and what you can guess about how people will respond to that, you can piece together a working hypothesis about how your business might find its place in the world of 5, 10, 20 years' time.

★★★

Although lean methodology has been popularised in recent years, the idea of experimentation can sit uneasily, especially among established businesses as opposed to start-ups unburdened by legacy systems and assumptions. Many businesses are still conditioned to seek and project certainty – which is why they process ever larger pools of data, produce ever more complex financial models, and look to management consultants for external validation of their ideas. They want to know what the evidence is, what the data supports, and to march into the annual meeting safe in the knowledge that they can claim to have done what the evidence most supported. This pursuit of certainty is enshrined in the shareholder-centric model, which requires companies to constantly win permission for their ideas from their investors, people who generally sit outside the everyday operations and realities. Shareholders crave predictable returns, and generally get restive when they are given anything other than a stable forecast for the next quarter.

The problem with this notion is that it's largely illusory, when so much is changing around every business, and it gets in the way of the flexible and experimental approach you need. Just as companies need to get away from unnecessary complexity in

how they think about change, they need to give up
on the phantom ideal of certainty, one that primarily
exists to be packaged up neatly for annual reports or
investor presentations. There are no absolute truths
or right answers on which you can build an ideal
business model, only things that you can pick up and
adopt through constant experimentation. In the same
way that behavioural science has taught us that
humans are not the wholly rational and logic-driven
creatures we once believed, we need to lose the notion
that everything in business can be reduced to bottom-
line calculations and financial models. These matter,
but they are not everything. Business is also about
subjectivity, unpredictable outcomes, and successes
against the odds. We need not just to leave room for
these things, but to embrace them as essential
ingredients.

Companies that want to successfully achieve change
need more than just access to capital, good ideas and
great people, important as all those things are. They
also need the mindset for change, and that is one
grounded in the constant business of experimentation,
where your guiding star is not the next quarter's targets
(although you will still have them) but what you are
learning from experiments about how to constantly
change and improve what you do. Experimentation
can't just be something that you do every now and
then: it has to be a central organising principle for your
business, one embedded in everyday thinking and
decision-making. A shift in mindset, from the quest for
certainty that has long been the corporate norm, to

the pursuit of constant experimentation and therefore the embrace of uncertainty, is one of the most important changes any business seeking a reboot needs to achieve.

CHAPTER 5

THE CULTURE

A focus on improvement and constant reinvention, a mindset rooted in experimentation, and judicious use of technology are all key ingredients of rebooting business. But the one thing that binds them together, which makes all of that possible and without which everything else becomes irrelevant, is having a brilliant team aligned around a shared set of values.

If experimentation provides the compass, and technology the engine, it is people who actually get behind the wheel and drive. The quality and commitment of the people on your team is what separates companies who accelerate into change from those who get left behind.

Great people are at the heart of every successful business, but that is especially true when you are trying to build one that operates on the basis of hypotheses and experimentation, rather than fixed objectives and planning. Just as it equips you with the flexibility to thrive in changing circumstances, experimentation demands that you organise in a more flexible way, with more people taking decisions and working autonomously. When you are in experimentation mode, you need to empower your employees to take the initiative all across a business. In a disorganised world, you do not win through strict organisation, but with a more unstructured approach that has the flexibility to change when the prevailing circumstances do. There is no room for bureaucracy and no time for the bottlenecks that hierarchy creates.

This is where culture becomes so important. In the environment every business now faces, traditional strategy and management are insufficient. You cannot fix in advance how you are going to cope with factors that are changing on such a constant basis, and others which are entirely unforeseeable. There is too much going on for the leadership of a business to take in, analyse and make decisions about. That is why you need decentralised, democratic structures, empowering people at all levels of seniority to come up with ideas and take decisions, putting the emphasis on those who are closest to everyday operations and customer problems. The only way this can work is if your culture is strong enough to bear the weight of this more distributed authority.

Culture fills the gaps and reaches the places that strategy and the leadership team cannot. It informs how people think about the challenges they and their teams face, and the way they work towards decisions. A company culture is something ephemeral that exists as mood music, but it is also an essential code, a yardstick to help people determine what is appropriate, desirable or sensible.

In a business that runs on experimentation, you are asking more people to make more decisions, more frequently, to avoid getting stuck. Culture is what allows the collective organisational brain to function in something like a unified fashion, allowing a multitude of different people to draw on the same fundamental assumptions and instincts. When the questions are constantly changing, no pre-ordained strategic manual is going to hold the answers you need, although strategy does of course set the frame for what you are trying to achieve. It is only in culture, which will evolve but should not fundamentally change, that the stable foundation to address a moving target can be found.

What makes a culture?

Every business has a culture. Culture can be about togetherness, ambition, self-improvement and achievement. It can equally be something that manifests itself in division, disaffection and an obsessive focus on politics over progress. Secrecy can be ingrained in a company culture as much as transparency. Cliques can be as much a product of culture as collaboration.

Culture matters hugely because it helps determine the people you will attract, as employees, customers, investors and advocates. How you behave as a company and the way you treat people determines the whole experience everyone has with your business. It defines whether the company is somewhere that people would recommend to their friends or is one where all relationships are fundamentally transactional and, as a result, transient. It permeates everything you do as a service provider, an employer, a client, supplier or partner.

You don't have a choice over whether your company has a culture, but you do have the ability to shape what that culture looks and feels like. When I arrived at Simply Business, the culture was not just hierarchical, but downright adversarial. Forcing people to wear suits and work strict hours was one thing; the stories I had heard about people needing to be restrained to stop fist fights around the boardroom table were an even starker sign that the atmosphere was in desperate need of repair. I remember walking through the door on my first day and thinking it felt more like a library than a start-up. There were around 50 people, sitting quietly in their separate teams, waiting to make sure they weren't the first person to leave for home. One person who precedes me remembers that the previous leadership would inspire the team with comments such as 'I can't hear any keyboards being typed'.

A culture is not something that a leader or senior team can manufacture in a petri dish and franchise across a business. But neither is it an entirely organic entity that emerges from the ether without conscious direction. You can facilitate a culture and, much as a gardener first plants and then tends their blooms, it needs constant attention in order to flourish.

That begins with having a clear idea about the kind of company, and therefore culture, you want to create. In our case, the ambition to become the first proper technology player in our industry set the terms of what we needed to achieve. For that to be possible, we were going to have to attract the very best technical talent, into an industry that wasn't an easy sell for developers.

It's also about having a group who will get behind what you are trying to do, and support the culture rather than undermining it. I'm not talking about communist election levels of endorsement, but an essential buy-in and agreement with the principles on which you are trying to build. You want people to think independently, to challenge and criticise, but to be with you on the essential direction of travel. The way I generally think about it is that scepticism is healthy but cynicism easily becomes corrosive.

That can mean hard choices. In my first year at Simply Business, I moved on 53 per cent of the workforce I inherited. This wasn't something I remotely enjoyed doing, but it was an important part of creating a stable foundation for what was to follow. The company I walked into was an unhappy one, with no CEO, a dysfunctional board and shareholder set, and a lot of people who frankly didn't really want to be there. Some didn't agree with what we wanted to do to effect change. Others weren't up to the job that we needed them to carry out. In the end, you need people who are going to fight with you rather than against you, and you cannot shy away from difficult decisions if you want to build a team that can embody a shared culture.

How else can you start to go about building a culture, whether it is from the ground up in a new business, or trying to engineer a graft in a company that has lost its way? There is certainly no question of anyone clicking their fingers and wishing a new way of working into being. You have to grow a culture, and that starts with planting the right seeds and hoping they take root. In practice, that means first you pick the things that matter to you, you create signifiers and symbols to make them tangible, then you keep tweaking and adding to them – increasingly driven by the collective view and reference – to reflect new conditions and changing circumstances. A useful way of thinking about company culture is the framework created by Edgar Schein, the management theorist and former MIT professor. He suggests that company culture operates at three levels: the unspoken assumptions shared by people within a company, the values that act as a shared guide to collective standards and conduct, and the 'artefacts and symbols' that help express those to people within as well as outside the company.

In developing a new culture at Simply Business, we might not have started out with clearly set values, but we have ended up focusing on three main things as our cultural touchstones, which have defined who we are and what we are about, and helped to attract and retain a consistently high-performing team of people. They are ambition, fun and openness.

Ambition

I did not come into the insurance industry expecting to be offering the promise of space travel, but that is exactly what I ended up doing in my first few months in the job. The first growth targets I set were wildly ambitious, and I didn't expect to achieve them. But it was important to make a statement of intent: we wanted to be a business on the move, and to become the best at what we were doing.

I didn't just set a high bar on metrics; I decided to do something different with the incentive too. Rather than promising everyone a pay rise (which we had plans to do anyway, unrelated to performance), I came up with a lottery. If we hit the targets that had been set, one person on our team would win a seat on the Virgin Galactic space mission. Unfortunately, those initial targets proved to be as elusive as commercial space travel so far has. We didn't send anyone to Mars, though two years later we did manage our first company trip abroad, to the distant metropolis of Brussels.

We might not have hit those first targets, and I might have disappointed the would-be astronauts on our team, but we had established something through that exercise. The only way was up, and fast.

Of course statements of ambition are one thing, but you need more than that to build a culture of ambition, where people come together to constantly move themselves, and the business, forward. To achieve that, you need to go beyond metrics. You need to do things that are in themselves ambitious, and which attract ambitious individuals to them. As the management author Dov Seidman has written: 'Leaders have to be purveyors of hope by giving people a journey that elevates them onto something that is worthy of their dedication … It's a move from exerting power over people to generating waves through them.'

In our business, a lot of that ambition was tied to the technology side. The rewrite of our entire platform, ditching a legacy code base to create something entirely new that would underpin our desire to continuously release upgrades, was a project that we could easily have balked at. By going ahead, hiring a visionary CTO who was both strategic and prepared to get elbow deep in the code base, we showed that we weren't going to let our ambition for the business be restricted by the technology base. It was an ambitious project, which we knew held the key to enabling us to do all the other things we wanted.

In parallel, our decision to use the Ruby on Rails coding language, uncommon then in web businesses, let alone the insurance industry, was another signifier of technical ambition, something designed to attract top talent and show we were not just an insurance company paddling in the shallow end of technology, but committed to becoming a serious development house. We set the bar not against our own industry, but at the best-in-class technology companies, with continuous deployment of updates where the insurance norm was monthly at best.

There were other, more obvious things we changed to signify that we wanted to be a proper technology company. When I arrived, people were working on lockdown computing systems that didn't allow them to access the Internet. The kit was outdated and clunky. It was the equivalent of saying, we want you do to industry-leading work but we're giving you only a hammer and chisel with which to do it. So we got rid of all of that, we gave people MacBooks, and we removed all limitations on use of the Internet.

An ambitious company is also about ambitious people and giving them the platform and opportunities to make progress in their careers. A business needs to be as ambitious for its employees as it is for itself. We've done this by pushing down responsibility as far as possible, letting those who are actually dealing with our technology systems and customers shape the experiments we try and the decisions we ultimately make.

When I look around the team we have, I don't just see a great group of people who work for this business, but many who are almost certainly going to start companies of their own at some point. I don't see that as a loss, or a threat, but a great thing. If the culture you have created allows people to fulfil their ambitions, nurse new ones and ultimately encourages them to go it alone to pursue them, then you can be sure not just that you have done a good thing, but that other brilliant people are going to come to fill the gaps. Strong culture is what ensures that what comes next is always at least as good as what has gone before. In a world where people, competitors, trends and technologies are constantly moving, it is the one thing above all that offers you stability.

Fun

After one of the several private equity deals we undertook prior to our eventual acquisition, our new investors put the management team through a psychological test called the Hogan Assessment. Part of this measures your personality against 10 defined values, to see what you most care about and are influenced by. Many of them are the standard sort of thing you would expect to see: power, altruism, security, commerce, tradition. The one we all scored through the roof on is a word you might not usually find in the business lexicon: hedonism.

I have to say, that made me smile when we were given the results. I'm not sure what our new investors thought, but by then they'd already signed the cheque.

We probably didn't need the confirmation that we are a bunch that likes to enjoy ourselves. That doesn't mean it's a 9 to 5, Monday to Friday, bacchanalian free-for-all. But it's definitely true that we have made having fun a core part of how we work together, not just beyond the office at the big awaydays, but in the everyday. In our annual lookalikes picture competition at Christmas, I have been given everyone from Willy Wonka to Claudio Ranieri and Joseph Stalin (the latter, I hope, due more to my tendency to wear my top button done up than my management style).

To continue the Russian theme, I am also the proud owner of a picture of my head mocked up onto the bare-chested torso of Vladimir Putin, riding an equally fictitious bear across a Russian lake. In fact I regard this as one of the most precious business trophies I own. There's a story behind it, which I'll get to, but the important thing is what it signifies. Because when it was presented to me, I knew we were doing something right; that the business had become one in which our people were more inclined to take the piss than to take me, or themselves, too seriously.

I can almost sense some of you starting to cringe at this point. Fun in the corporate environment can be crass, it can be forced and something that certain people will actively run a mile from. There are few more terror-inducing phrases in the English language than 'organised fun'. And, of course, what to one person is a great joke can be hurtful and upsetting to another.

You need to be careful about how you go about it. And you need to respect the needs and requirements of your whole team, not just the extroverts. But to be honest, you also need to make sure your team enjoy their work and get plenty of opportunities to let their hair down. We spend so much time at work, with colleagues rather than friends or family, that it's pretty miserable to imagine it involving no fun at all. While much of that enjoyment comes from doing work you find interesting, motivating and challenging, it's probably not enough to expect that people will find all the enrichment they need from the day job alone. And there is no inherent conflict between people having a good time and doing good work. An informal business can also be a deadly serious one. If you're less stuffy, it can help you take the edge off the reality of hard business challenges, setting a sustainable pace and building an ethos that is authentic and fun.

There are two things we do to try and instil a culture of fun within the company: one is about what goes on inside the business, and another takes place entirely outside office walls.

At work, we run hackathons, in the same way as lots of tech companies. These are sessions that last a couple of days: we start with a theme, people pitch outline ideas, form teams to explore and develop them, and we vote on a winner at the end. There's both a silly and a serious part to this. We've got a beer bot that delivers drinks to desks, and a drone that can be controlled by playing a guitar, two of many weird and wonderful inventions that emerged from company hackathons. We've also developed products and systems that we use in the business: from our telephony system, to the project on which we have based our plan for a four-day working week.

The hackathons are freeform time, where people get to play with technologies and ideas that might have some bearing on what we do in the business, or which might not. It's another, less structured and more long-term, form of the experimentation I have already talked about. And it's great fun: people working on ambitious projects to short deadlines, presenting back their impressive successes and equally dramatic failures, and having a good laugh doing it. It's people doing what they are good at, and interested in, but without the constraints and demands of the day job. It's also an opportunity, as we frequently do, to bring in outside consultants and advisors to push our thinking and offer new ideas.

Your accountant would tell you how many hours you lose out of the business by giving people a few days a year in which to mess around, but the upside in terms of goodwill and new ideas is so much greater. In fact, so successful have the hackathons been that we are currently experimenting with how we can embed the ethos and approach into the everyday operations of the business. We want hackathon-driven development – with all the energy, idea-generation, experimentation and fun that comes with it – to become core to how we work the whole time, not just for a few days a year.

Some of the things you can do to instil a culture of fun are directly related to the business, and can have a knock-on positive impact (though you shouldn't expect or mandate that). But of course, if you want people to really enjoy themselves, and to have something to look forward to, nothing beats throwing a massive party.

In my second year, we started talking about how we could up the ante on that front, and maybe take some of the team abroad. The first idea discussed among the management team was that we could do a trip of a lifetime for around 20 of the top performers. That led to a conversation about what we could do for the whole team. In year one, that meant going to about the closest possible place which could be considered overseas, which was Brussels, via Eurostar. We did it on the cheap, but it went down brilliantly and the stories were a bit wilder than you might expect from an event held in a café in the otherwise deserted (at the weekend) business district. In the intervening years we've ramped things up quite a bit, and our most recent trip saw us charter a 747 aircraft to Berlin, stay in five-star accommodation and hire out an entire nightclub overlooking the city.

The total cost of subsiding a three-day trip for several hundred, although not as much per head as you might expect, is another thing that will have the bean counters climbing the walls. It helps that we have a finance team that is as much at the heart of the experiences as any other team within the business. The big moments are an investment, rewarding people for their hard work, creating a centrepiece occasion where we all come together outside the office environment, and nurturing goodwill that can last long after the hangovers have subsided.

You might argue that if we're going to spend a bunch of money on something like that, shouldn't we just divide it up and give everyone their share to spend as they please? Which is a perfectly fair point, but I would argue that it wouldn't help you to build a culture and feeling of togetherness. People will thank you for a spot bonus, but they won't remember that conversation in the same way as they will a kicking night out with plenty more to come. In this I was influenced by the thinking of the behavioural scientists Elizabeth Dunn and Michael Norton, who in their book *Happy Money* talk about shared experiences as one of the keys to increased happiness. I believe in making sure everyone on our teams shares in our success, which is why we have given equity to everyone, and a pay rise every year as well. But I also think that lived experiences as a team can achieve something financial incentives alone do not. If you want to create a culture that will sustain you through the good times and the tough ones, you need to do things together as much as you reward people independently. As we grow, it becomes more important than ever that there are things we still do as one team.

When I'm asked what the most important priorities for a leader are, not running out of money is always near the top of the list. However, you have to spend money as well as manage it, and while expenditure on your team and your culture might feel frivolous to some, it is as good an investment for your long-term prospects as any other. If you want your people to spend their precious time and lend their expertise to your cause, then make sure you are willing to spend some money on them too.

Openness

'You won't always agree with everything I say, but I promise I'll tell you the truth and you can make up your own mind what you think of it.' This was something I said to the team very early on, and I've done everything I can since to stick to it. Because if you want to build the kind of business I have talked about, there is no room for institutionalised secrecy, variable information, and leaving people guessing. There are some things, notably fundraising deals, that you keep a close circle around for good reasons. And if I've made mistakes on this front, it has typically been through sharing too much rather than too little. But on the whole, in the vast majority of circumstances, a business where the culture is open, information is shared, and people are brought into the circle of trust is one that stands a better chance of succeeding, especially in the face of uncertainty and change.

Being open is something that has been fundamentally important to our culture since the beginning, and it is significant on a number of different levels. At its most fundamental level, it means we are open to everyone, from all sorts of places and backgrounds, and with a weird and wonderful range of interests. The meeting rooms in our office are named after some of the places where our team grew up, from Grimsby (me, in case I haven't mentioned that yet) to Elbistan (southern Turkey) and other glamorous locales such as Milton Keynes.

Our team was once described to me by a senior figure in the industry as a 'bunch of weirdos'. It was meant as a compliment and taken as one. We pride ourselves on being open to everyone who wants to join us, as long as they have the skills for the job and want to add in their own way to the collective ethos and culture. That includes unusual people who might not be an obvious fit for the role or the industry. We want the polymaths, the people with unusual life stories and professional experiences, and individuals who might feel they don't naturally have a place elsewhere. This means we have people with degrees ranging from pharmacology to zoology. One of our team is an amateur historian who leads walking tours of London in his spare time; another was a club DJ who would occasionally fly off to Brazil for the weekend for a gig.

You don't build a strong business on a narrow base of personalities, life experiences and expertise. Our strength as a team has always been in embracing people's idiosyncrasies and differences, and creating an environment where everyone can be themselves, not some persona they project only for work purposes. We do skew quite heavily towards those who like gaming, and my favourite-ever introduction to an internal presentation was by one of our product team whose opening gambit was: 'The only thing you really need to know about me is that I roleplay an elf in World of Warcraft.'

A culture of openness is also essential to building the trust you need to power a business that seeks constant improvement, runs on the basis of contin-uous experimentation, and affords people a high level of autonomy to facilitate that. You need trust to run not just downwards from the leadership, but sideways across teams and between people. If a business is incapable of running on trust, between people at all levels, it's probably also incapable of doing most of the things I am talking about here. Trust is the catalyst for almost everything a business needs to do to adapt and thrive in a world of uncertainty, where a prescriptive, hierarchical way of running companies no longer holds water. When you don't have trust, you haven't got a hope of building an open, honest and collaborative business culture where people face up to the challenges of unknowns and uncertainty, admit to each other what they don't know, and engage in constant experimentation, much of which will fail.

That is why, in common with many companies who run agile processes, most of our teams take part in daily stand-up meetings to run through the status of different work streams, and to surface and discuss any problems. We have wider sessions for the whole team at less frequent intervals, to discuss projects and progress in the round. It was at one of these all-hands meetings that a developer, then quite new to the team, volunteered that he had broken something in the code base. And then, in trying to fix it, he had broken it again. It took a lot of bravery to stand up in front of a few hundred people and admit to having got something wrong, not just once but twice. For me it was quite rewarding to hear, because it showed the culture of openness at work. Now, if someone is getting things wrong the whole time, then you have to question if they are the right person for the job. But unless the culture supports people to admit when things have gone wrong, and to ask for help in putting them right, you are never going to create the permission for a truly experimental environment. That is the only way to build a better business for customers: by consistently testing new ideas, including many that are doomed to fail.

People can have an antipathy to showing any vulnerability in the work environment, but when they are willing to do so, you know the culture of mutual trust and support is there. So while I always like to hear when things are going well, I'm equally happy to be told that mistakes have been made and experiments have failed, as long as it is accompanied by an assessment of what we've learned and decided to do as a result. Positive news about record-breaking levels of tractor production can only take you so far. You also need to know where the problems are, and what roadblocks are being encountered. It takes a lot of trust for people to share their fears and concerns, allowing more people to work on a problem. But when you are moving fast to constantly experiment, there is no alternative. It is our culture of openness that helps ingrain the trust that is such a central part of how we operate.

Culture in action

Culture is something you can do much to nurture and encourage, but it's not until you start to see it in action that you know whether those efforts have worked or not. It is the small things that prove, often during difficult moments, that the culture has moved beyond an idea that existed in a few people's heads and has become something that informs the way people think and behave within the business.

One example that sticks in my mind is when the first private equity deal I had put together fell apart, after over a year's worth of work. Within a few months, I had put together a new deal with another investor and was ready to take it to the board. I had made up my mind: either they would agree to it, and the terms on which we wanted to buy them out, or I would resign. I was going into the meeting with our COO, my closest partner in rebuilding and growing the business. Shortly before we were due to start, I told him that I planned to quit on the spot if the shareholders spiked the deal. His response was to walk back to his desk, and write a resignation letter of his own, ready for the same eventuality.

When you have a strong culture, you find it asserting itself when it is needed most, which generally means when you hit a snag of some sort. When we decided to do the platform rebuild I have described, our shareholders were putting us under significant time pressure. They wanted it delivered within a three-month time frame, which was pushing things, to put it politely. The upshot was a huge amount of time pressure was placed on the whole team. It was at an all-hands meeting, sharing this unhappy news, that I started to use the perhaps doomed metaphor of the bear to describe our predicament. I said our legacy code base was like this horrible, massive bear that we just had to wrestle to the ground, however much effort it took. Then our CTO chipped in, tongue in cheek. 'No,' he said. 'The legacy platform is a whale, trying to eat the pod of dolphins on which we are trying to escape.' So we held a vote, Project Dolphin beat Project Bear, and now you know the story of how my head became better acquainted with Vladimir Putin's body and imaginary bear-riding antics. (Incidentally, when I showed my then four-year-old daughter the picture all she could say was, 'Dad, wasn't you cold with your shirt off?')

That could have been a very difficult meeting, because we were essentially telling people that they had to get used to the idea of working a lot harder for the next few months. But they responded with humour, didn't take the situation too seriously and showed the perspective you need to cope with major challenges: a recognition that, in the end, it's not a life or death situation, just some work that needs to be done, even if there is quite a lot of it to do.

The culture I have described has provided the backbone for the agile, experimental business we wanted to build. The focus on ambition has helped bring in brilliant individuals with their own ideas, who enjoy working in an environment where we are always trying to change and improve things. The emphasis on fun and informality has helped us get through the difficult moments that any business seeking change will often face. And the openness we have encouraged has created an environment where people trust each other enough to be brutally honest, in a way that you have to be when you are constantly changing things and will often break something before you make it work better.

Nothing I have described so far about how to pursue and achieve change within a business is easy. And change can only be achieved if you nurture a team of people who actually work together, share the desire to be part of a working environment that is centred on change, and are willing to take on more responsibility to generate ideas and make decisions. That is why, as much as you need to be thinking about how customer needs are changing, how technology can help you to meet those, and what experiments you can put in place to make that happen, you need to invest equal commitment in the team who will deliver all those things, and the culture that will help them to do so.

PART III

Rebooting leadership

'The best teacher lodges an intent not in the mind but in the heart.'

Anne Michaels, *Fugitive Pieces*

CHAPTER 6

GIVE BACK CONTROL

'Do you care to know why I'm in this chair, why I earn the big bucks? I'm here for one reason and one reason alone. I'm here to guess what the [market] might do a week, a month, a year from now. That's it, nothing more.'

This wasn't my speech to the business on the first day I joined.

The person who did say it was a bit more smartly dressed, has considerably more hair, and is probably a better public speaker: Jeremy Irons.

In the movie *Margin Call*, a dramatisation of the beginning of the 2008 financial crisis, the board of an investment bank (a lightly fictionalised Lehman Brothers) is having a crisis meeting. The CEO, played by Irons, lands his helicopter on the helipad and swoops in to chair the meeting, where he is told for the first time his company is holding a potentially fatal volume of junk securities on its balance sheet. He then delivers the speech quoted above, before declaring that the game is over, and, against the protests of his trading chief, ordering a fire sale of the toxic assets.

It's a perfect characterisation of a certain style of business leadership that was once the norm: where power and decision-making were concentrated in the hands of an individual prized for his or her ability to sniff the air and pluck out a strategy. It's the grand-master view of business: a single, star player with responsibility for seeing the whole board and moving their pawns around accordingly.

The problem with this approach in today's world is it has become akin to trying to play chess while wearing a blindfold. If it was ever possible for one person to see the whole picture for their business, sector and indeed the market as a whole, that time is long gone. The pace of change, the complexity of factors at play, and the sheer volume of information mean it is not only undesirable to try and funnel decision-making through a single channel, but simply impractical.

If you want to build the kind of experimental and culture-powered business I have described, then this old concept of leadership deserves to be thrown out of the highest-floor boardroom window you can find. Forget the grand, heroic visions of being rain-maker, recruiter, soothsayer and strategist rolled into one. Consider instead your role as being an enabler and a facilitator: bringing together the best possible team and creating the conditions for them to thrive, as I discussed in the previous chapter. Giving people responsibility that empowers them, while shouldering the burden of problems that would inhibit them. Setting a tone and pointing the way forward, but letting others decide their own interpretation of how to get there. More orchestra conductor than vistuoso soloist.

I am not saying that the necessity for good leadership has gone away. In fact, good leadership is probably more important than ever as companies respond to the necessity for change, but our definition of what that is needs to change too. A good leader in today's world isn't just looking at what they can personally influence or make happen; they are working to build a business that, in its everyday operations, effectively functions without them. You have to write yourself out of the script, because being in it all of the time is simply too laborious, time-consuming and inefficient for the current business environment.

When our COO, who left the UK team to lead the launch of the US business, told me shortly after his departure was announced that he was surprised the team had moved on so quickly, I had to point out that this was actually something of a tribute. He had done such a good job in hiring a brilliant group of people, and setting them off on a clear trajectory, that in many ways his influence was no longer needed. It would be superhuman not to feel conflicted in these instances, but as a leader your aim should be to reach a point where your team doesn't feel your absence when you're gone. As Tim O'Reilly quotes General Stanley McChrystal, in his book *WTF*: 'I tell people, "Don't follow my orders. Follow the orders I would have given you if I were there and knew what you know."'

The reboot in leadership that our business climate demands is one in which bosses accept a role where deference is much less but the demands are arguably greater. It's about giving away power and control without shirking responsibility for big decisions; being humble while remaining decisive; and facing up to the very stark decisions that every business must take in a world defined by change and uncertainty. In particular, there are four things existing and aspiring leaders should be thinking about in order to build more experimental and culturally robust companies that are capable of thriving through change. You need to give as way as much responsibility as you can to other people, focus on building a high-trust environment, make sure you shoulder the burden of tough decisions that only you can make, and maintain a keen level of self-awareness about how others see you.

i) Give away responsibility

I often say, there are several hundred people in my organisation, I don't know where they are today, and I don't really care. That's not just because we believe in flexible working. It also reflects my basic belief that these individuals are the best judges of when, where and how they can best do their work.

This reflects my basic attitude towards leadership – which is, the less I get involved, usually the better. When you first take on a leadership role, it's tempting to try and get your hands on everything that's going on, to be a party to all key decisions and make sure you have the final say. You want to do everyone else's job for them because you think you can do it better (and in some cases that might be true). That isn't just unsustainable for you as an individual, it's crippling for collective morale and people's individual sense of ownership over their decisions.

The logical conclusion of a fast-paced business environment is that you simply can't keep on top of everything that's going on. Even if you wanted to, you couldn't. My advice is that you shouldn't want to. Herb Kelleher, the founder and long-time CEO of US carrier Southwest Airlines, which he helped grow from a regional-focused start-up into one of the world's largest airlines, put it very well when he said: 'A financial analyst once asked me if I was afraid of losing control of our organization. I told him I've never had control and I never wanted it. If you create an environment where people have to truly participate you don't need control.'

He puts his finger on an important truth for any business leader: in a world full of questions, the people who are closest to the answers are those nearest to you. Whether you're trying to work out how to take advantage of a new technology, deal with a threatening trend or competitor, rebuild some part of your platform or product offering, or rewire some aspect of your culture or working practice, the best people to help guide those decisions are often in your own team. Democratising the process by which you develop new ideas, experiment with them, and decide what to proceed with is not only the most engaging way to build a business in uncertain times but also the most effective. It road tests and stress tests your assumptions against the practical knowledge, experience and insight of the people who are often much closer to the everyday business realities than their bosses. And it takes decisions about new tools and technologies away from those at the top of an organisation, who may be remunerated the highest but are often least well equipped to under-stand the changing environment we face and how to respond.

Many executives, especially in established compa-nies, will be past the tipping point once famously identified by the author Douglas Adams, when we start seeing new inventions as more troublesome than transformative. So you need to make sure there is a flow of ideas from people who are engaging with emerging technologies as a default, rather than those who may feel distant from them.

Giving away responsibility, and empowering people to develop ideas and make decisions independently isn't just about spreading goodwill and promoting engagement, although it can achieve both those things. And it's not just about letting you focus on the things that matter most, although it can help with that too. It's fundamentally about how a business has to operate in an age of constant change and information saturation. When the headwinds are this strong, a top-heavy company is going to overbalance, because too small a part of the organisation is trying to take responsibility for too many things. Instead you need to focus on hiring the very best people, creating flexibility and bench-strength, and having a democratised, decentralised structure where responsibility is shared as widely as possible. You need to keep in mind something that has been clear to me since I worked in a call centre during my twenties: traditional management is a failure of leadership, which should not be about controlling but empowering; giving people the tools to work with, rather than instructions to follow to the letter.

So how do you give away responsibility without creating a free-for-all from which no coherent strategy can emerge? This is where the careful balance of good leadership comes in: providing direction that aligns people's efforts without prescribing or limiting how they pursue the agreed goals. Giving people responsibility and authority is important, but unless it is allied to a clear sense of overall strategy and mission, you are never going to create a coherent team and organisation where people's efforts complement rather than contradict each other.

A thriving business in a changing world is a delicate thing. It has to be flexible enough to cope with change, while being sufficiently focused that chaos does not ensue. It requires authority to be dispersed, but with a strong enough core to hold everything together. And it needs, if not a script for teams to read off, then strong enough guidelines and guide ropes to keep everyone moving in the same direction and towards the same goals.

Giving away responsibility is difficult, not because of some issue of pride, but because it requires even greater discipline from leaders to get the balance right between pointing the way forward and getting out of the way to let others lead. Interfere too much and you risk disenfranchising the exact spirit and culture you are trying to nurture; while if you give too little direction, people start looking around wondering whether the captain is asleep at the wheel.

How to square the circle? My first rule of thumb is don't interfere on a decision that you know could be handled effectively by someone else without your input. You also shouldn't countermand someone else's decision, unless you are entirely convinced it is damaging or counter-cultural (and if that is happening a lot, you have to ask yourself whether the people themselves are right). Thirdly, if you know you have to be party to a particular decision (for example approving a new ad campaign), don't wait until the last minute to give your view. Be a part of the process early on, give feedback, and help shape the development rather than waiting to sit in judgment on a final product. If you are going to be involved in something, be willing to get your hands dirty. And if you're not, just let it go.

By doing this you make the whole organisation into a team of leaders, with people directing their own activity and resources at the most appropriate things. Your role as a leader then becomes more about monitoring progress and stepping in to make adjustments if absolutely necessary, rather than trying to direct and control everything from above.

ii) Focus on trust

I mentioned in the last chapter how important trust is in underpinning an open, collaborative and experimental business culture. Leaders have an essential role to play in facilitating this.

It starts with your own behaviour, whether you are the ultimate boss or running a division or project team. The signals you send, and the trust you show, will set the tone for everyone else. If you are checking in on people's work in a way that suggests you don't expect it to be delivered on time or done well, then you can be absolutely certain that behaviour will repeat itself across your team. And if it does, then you have something that is more surveillance state than smooth-running business.

To build trust, you need to start by showing it. In recruitment decisions, for instance, I see my job as hiring the person who hires the team in a given part of the business. I want to have faith that we have the right person in place, someone in tune with our values, who understands the business challenges, and whose judgement I trust. Once I have helped decide who that person should be, I will never make a hiring decision for them, or interfere in any recruitment matter unless asked to. If I do, I'm not only signalling my lack of trust in that individual, but in my own decision to hire them in the first place. There can't be many worse things a leader can do than recruit someone to do a job and then not give them the space or authority to actually do it. If a leader can't show trust in their people, they can't complain if no one else does either.

One of the best examples was when our CTO came to me six months into a major project to replace our telephony system. We were already behind schedule; despite that, his advice was not to speed up but slow down. He wanted to down tools for a month and experiment with an entirely different approach, one he thought could ultimately get us the desired result more quickly, even if it meant losing more time in the short term. It was essentially admitting that we had made a bad call at the outset, and would now delay an already behind-schedule, business-critical project in search of something better. As things turned out, it was the right decision. The second choice proved better than the first would have been. We were only able to get to that point because of the trust in each other: from our CTO that I wouldn't throw my toys out of the pram about a further delay, and from me that we should back his instinct and expertise, even though it cut across what we had been working on for half a year. Decisions like that are only possible when you trust those you are working with implicitly.

It's easy to talk about giving trust, and sign up to the notion in principle, but the acid test is when someone on your team wants to do something you disagree with. While there are times when you can step in, argue the case, or even sometimes enforce your opinion, you can't do that all the time. And you should only try when you are utterly convinced that a serious mistake is about to be made. On many other occasions, while you can have the discussion, you need to let people go with their own gut instinct. You can't have it both ways: seeking to create an environment of mutual trust while also trying to hold on to all the decisions.

Beyond your own individual behaviour, you also have to work on making sure your team trust each other, especially those who hold management positions. When I started at Simply Business, dealing with trust among the management team was one of the worst problems we faced. Senior managers didn't trust their counterparts, or their teams, to do the job properly. We had one or two management meetings that descended into shouting matches, and afterwards people would split off into small groups, clearly to discuss the outcome of the meeting. Bear in mind this was all happening in glass-fronted meeting rooms, transmitted directly to anyone on the team who cared to look.

The challenge with trust is that people almost never raise the issue directly. You won't find many saying, 'I don't trust that person.' They're more likely to cast aspersions on their competence, punctuality or attitude. The problem is one of trust, but it's so often masked and presented under a different, less obviously subjective guise. In our case, the proxy issue was timekeeping: there were endless gripes about this team coming in late, that one leaving early and so on. It was the most obvious source of distrust in the business, but no one was thinking about it in those terms.

So I initiated an experiment, creating three different sets of hours (0830–1630, 0930–1730 and 1030–1830) that people could choose to work. This didn't in itself solve the issue, but it did allow us to show that the problem was less one of timekeeping (because people could come and go with the greater flexibility we had introduced) and more one of a lack of trust, especially about other people's teams. Once we had established an agreement that the problem was trust, we were in a better position to address it directly.

There are also some simple things you can do to facilitate trust in the everyday life of a business. In some of our team meetings, we will begin not with the business priorities but with space for people to share what's going on in their personal lives, good and bad. It's an exercise lifted from the global CEO network YPO, where you score your energy levels in the three areas of your life: personal, business and family, talking about what you've been doing and how you've been feeling in those three areas since the previous meeting. People will often be surprisingly frank about some of the issues and challenges they are facing, the sorts of things they might not normally be comfortable raising in the work environment. This is important on a number of levels: it bonds groups and helps encourage greater tolerance for each other as people, all facing our own different challenges. As a leader, it can also help you to help people who might be going through a tough time. If you know, for example, that one of your team is going through a divorce or relationship breakdown, it's that much easier to make the allowances and concessions they may need in their working life.

Building trust is not something that happens quickly. By definition it can only emerge from people working closely together, often in testing circumstances, and learning about each other's strengths, weaknesses and idiosyncrasies. Trust can only come where people are open to it, and when any emerging sources of distrust are nipped in the bud.

Because the kind of experimental, democratised business I am talking about relies so much on trust, one of your most important tasks as a leader – at any level – is to promote a high-trust environment and protect it at all costs. That begins with your own behaviour, it extends into how your management team operates, and it is ultimately fulfilled in the experience that every single member of your team has. Promoting trust can mean sacrificing your right to have the final say, and it requires considerable self-discipline to avoid interfering in a way that undermines people and erodes trust. It's worth the effort: the collective benefits of building trust are much greater than any personal costs. And when you really do trust that your team is going to do the best possible job, you get the greatest prize for any leader in business: having one less thing to worry about.

iii) Hold on to burdens

So far I have talked mostly about aspects of the traditional leadership spec you need to discard, and the authority you need to give away. That said, there are still things that only a leader can and should be responsible for. Because however flat your hierarchy and however decentralised your decision-making, some questions, decisions and priorities need to be shouldered by the individual with whom the buck ultimately stops. Just as you have to give away plenty of authority, there are certain areas of responsibility that you cannot and should not seek to delegate.

Most often these are to do with money, whether you are raising it or at risk of running out of it. When you are down to your last £20k, as Simply Business was in my first couple of months as CEO, you don't call a public vote to decide what to do next. And when you are negotiating a fundraising of some kind, you don't go and tell everyone about it until everything is ready to go. Or at least you shouldn't. I learned that lesson when doing our first private equity deal. For most of my first year in the job, I had been working to put together a deal with an investor I knew, to buy out the muddle of shareholders I had inherited and provide a much-needed injection of capital.

At the point I thought we had it all confirmed, we told the whole management team. Then, when it fell apart in the final confirmation meeting, we were left with nothing from a year of work, and more people uncertain about the future than would have been the case had I kept the cards closer to my chest. At that point I had a choice: either resign or try and put together another deal. So, without telling anyone except our COO, I approached some new investors and started to build an alternative. This time, it was only when the ink had dried that we shared the news with the whole team.

This was one of the most important things I learned from my early leadership experience: not to lightning rod the pressures I was feeling down into the team and the business as a whole. When you are dealing with financial issues that can be make or break for a business, you need to be prudent about what you tell to who and when. During the deal that fell through, it was obvious that the process was putting a huge strain on those involved in it, distracting them from the day job of keeping the business moving forward. In retrospect, telling the whole management team a deal was done before everything had been double-confirmed was the wrong move. Transparency is important, but if you give people information they can't do anything with, which adds to the stress they feel day-to-day, you aren't helping anyone. A big part of your job as a leader is to take on those pressures, so others have the space to do their job properly, without feeling the strain of worrying about issues over which they have no control.

You want a democratised organisation, where decisions are taken by those closest to them, and people feel empowered to shape their own path. That does not mean a company should be a wholesale democracy, where everyone knows everything, information flows without restriction, and people are worrying about things that are well outside their job spec. Where people can contribute ideas, expertise and insight into debates about the future of the business, experiments on products and customer services, and company culture, then you should spread the discussion as widely as possible. But when a pressing question is going to cause more angst than it sheds light, then you gain nothing by making more people worry about it.

A good leader today will give away much more information and authority than was the case historically, but they will also know what to hold on to, and when to make sure the pressure they are feeling over a big decision does not transfer itself onto the wider team. Ultimately you need to think about letting power go, while keeping hold of responsibility.

iv) Understand how you are seen

The last thing you need to remember when you're the boss, however enlightened, democratic and focused on empowering others you are, is that you are still the boss. And that is how your team sees you. How you behave on a day-to-day basis isn't only important in direct interactions; it matters in everything visible that you do. People often talk about the fear of having the boss peering over their shoulder, looking at what's on their screen (and even though I tell people all the time I don't care if they are on Twitter or Instagram, you still see people reflexively closing browser tabs as you approach), but the reality is that a CEO or manager has only one pair of eyes, and their team has dozens or even hundreds. As a leader, no one is being scrutinised and judged more than you. People notice and assess things that you wouldn't believe they would pay the slightest bit of attention to. On my first day at Simply Business, I introduced myself to the team in a series of small meetings, and was later told that I had made an impression just because I was dressed casually in jeans, and perched on the side of a table to talk rather than standing at the front of the room to deliver a slide presentation. Those small things alone signalled that things were going to be different from that point, and that needless formality was out.

At other times I've been guilty of creating a negative impression, by not being sufficiently aware of how I come across to others. I've had to work hard at being self-contained in how I react to things, especially problems. If you leave a difficult meeting with a face like thunder, the people who see you are going to pick up on that, talk about it, and quite possibly speculate about the reasons why. If someone approaches you to ask something, and you respond snappily because you've been distracted from something more immediately important, that interaction of a few seconds can leave a long-term negative impression. On no account can you dump the pressures you are feeling onto the next person who tries to talk to you. It might feel cathartic, but it's also a toxic way to behave, and it undermines your relationships and the culture you are trying to build. You have to learn to control your emotions and your body language, to recognise that you are on show in the working environment and beyond, and be rigorously self-aware about the way you behave and relate to others.

What time you come into work and leave the office, how you behave if you go down the pub, and your general demeanour in meetings and around the workplace are all things that your team will observe and draw conclusions from. If you habitually stay late, for instance, it can make people uncomfortable about leaving the office on time themselves. While in terms of extra-curricular activity I remember an old boss who I respected for his professional abilities but whose behaviour after a few drinks I did not admire. Over time that started to negatively affect how I saw him at work too; it becomes hard to separate one from the other.

As a leader you need to have the self-discipline to make sure what you do outside of office hours, and

even just your general demeanour in everyday dealings, doesn't undermine the values you are trying to
instil. On the whole that means you're better putting
your card behind the bar than leading the charge to
it. Symbols are an important piece of the picture, too.
I don't have an office, or even a fixed place where I
sit. We have a hot-desking arrangement, and like
anyone else I grab the nearest berth available when
I come in every morning. Even a tiny thing, like a
Post-it note stuck on a desk saying it's reserved for
me, can erode the ethos I have always believed in.
Everything you do and every choice you make as a
leader is a symbol, and it either supports the kind of
business you are trying to build, or detracts from it.

As a leader you can't create and sustain a culture
alone, but you can single-handedly undermine it if
your actions and behaviour cut against the grain of
what you talk about in team meetings. If you're trying
to nurture a strong culture, create an attractive working
environment and build a purposeful business, then as
leader you have an essential role in not just setting
the direction, but living and representing the values.
You have to be self-aware to make sure that, even if
inadvertently, you don't start to unpick the very things
you are trying to achieve.

***

There is a paradoxical side to the kind of leadership
needed to build successful companies in a changing
world. In many ways, it's about creating a more

liberating environment, one where people feel free to choose what they work on, and when and where they work. Free to put forward ideas, conduct experiments, and admit when they don't know something or that a mistake has been made. And free to call out things that aren't working and which need to change.

But creating those freedoms requires significant discipline, especially on the part of leaders. You need to be judicious about when to share problems and when to hold on to them; rigorous about making sure the decisions you make don't cut across the culture you are trying to enshrine; and self-disciplined in your personal behaviour, conscious about how everything you say and do is seen by others.

Good leadership is conscious of where it is needed, but most importantly where it isn't. And good leaders recognise that decisions and projects that run without them are a better sign of success than those which require heavy intervention. They show that the business is running under its own steam, that the people involved are the right ones, and the systems you have in place are working.

In a more complex and fast-changing business landscape, the onus of leadership is shifting from the things an individual leader or small leadership group does themselves, to the conditions they create that allow others to do more. When you are seeing and influencing less of what goes on, you need a business that is more autonomous both by instinct and design. You need to set a tone and a direction, one that gives people structure while affording them flexibility in how they operate; and you need to establish a series of common understandings that allow people to answer their own questions and develop their own projects. With those things in place, one of your most important jobs is then to get out of the way.

CHAPTER 7

TAKE RESPONSIBILITY

'We didn't take a broad enough view of our responsibility, and that was a big mistake. It was my mistake, and I'm sorry.'

That apology formed part of Mark Zuckerberg's written testimony prior to his appearance before the US Congress in April 2018, when he was called to explain a series of scandals surrounding Facebook, from its approach to data protection and user privacy, to how its platform was being exploited to spread fake news, extreme content and even potentially to interfere in democratic elections.

It was a far cry from how Zuckerberg first responded to suggestions that Facebook had been hijacked by outside forces to influence the outcome of the 2016 US Presidential election. That, he said at the time, was a 'crazy idea'. Ten months later, he was apologising for those comments in the wake of a Congressional inquiry into the matter. A little over a year later, he was announcing sweeping changes to the very foundation of Facebook, tilting the emphasis away from brand and news content and back towards friends' updates and family photographs. Then came the allegation that Cambridge Analytica, a data mining and analysis consultancy, had improperly accessed the personal information of up to 87 million Facebook users. Then an admission from Facebook that 2 billion of its users could conceivably have had personal information, including email addresses and phone numbers, scraped from their accounts. And finally, the wider acceptance that Facebook had failed in its duty, lost the trust of many of its users, and had to do better.

Facebook has been far from alone in experiencing a rude awakening amid growing scrutiny of technology companies' ethics and business practices. Uber, the symbolic company for both the Dr Jekyll and the Mr Hyde faces of Silicon Valley, has been through a similar rollercoaster of repentance and recantation. Under the leadership of its founder Travis Kalanick, with a bare-knuckle approach to competitors and authorities, a ruthless corporate culture that was damagingly exposed, and allegations stretching from corporate espionage to using software that evades law enforcement, the ride-hailing app seemed to test almost to destruction the idea that the balm of a cheaper and quicker service could soothe all other ills. Yet with major cities including London and Vancouver clamping down on the service, and hundreds of thousands of users joining a viral campaign to delete their Uber accounts, they found that there is a price to pay for being seen as unethical.

As Dara Khosrowshahi, who took over as CEO from Kalanick in the heat of these battles, said early in his tenure: 'The truth is that there is a high cost to a bad reputation … it really matters what people think of us, especially in a global business like ours, where actions in one part of the world can have serious consequences in another.'

He was reflecting a truth that, if it hasn't already become apparent, is rapidly dawning in company boardrooms: it's not just the product or service you sell, and the balance sheet you show to investors, that matter. How the sausage has been made is just as important. Just as people want to know where their food comes from, they want to know how the businesses they buy from and work for behave and operate: do they remunerate their employees fairly, do they pay their fair share of taxes, do they try and limit their environmental footprint?

The responsibilities facing business have increased, the bar for trust has been set much higher, and that is a fact of life companies need to get comfortable with. In a more globalised, connected and conscious business environment, with complex supply chains, customers in faraway places, and often a more flexible and dispersed workforce, the footprint of an average business is far less predictable and more prone to unknown or unpredictable factors than was the case even a decade ago.

That does not mean you can escape responsibility for it. A supermarket cannot simply say it didn't know that its suppliers were providing ready meals that said they were beef but actually turned out to contain horsemeat. Platform businesses cannot pretend they have no responsibility for the actions of their users, whether that is uploading extreme content or discriminating against other users. Gig economy employers cannot claim they have no responsibility for their workers, or even try to deny that they are their workers at all, as a series of court judgements have shown.

This combination of changing conditions – from growing scrutiny of how companies behave to increasing expectations on what they will stand for – represents a fundamental challenge to leaders. The work you do as a leader to build a thriving business is only half the job; in this more scrutinised, politicised and febrile environment for business, the way you do that has become just as important. You have to win the trust of consumers and employees to win their long-term loyalty, and that means answering more questions and meeting more expectations than was ever the case before.

It is true that few businesses are going to find themselves in the situation the likes of Uber and Facebook have. But the shape of the challenge is the same even where the scale is not: as a leader you are now more accessible to customers than at any time in the past; you are more publicly accountable for your own behaviour and that of your company; and you are subject to increased expectations of the ethical and environmental standards every company should meet.

If business is going to rebuild the trust that has been eroded in recent years, then leaders have an essential role to play in rising to these new challenges of trust and transparency. Doing so will mean embracing a whole new set of responsibilities that are starting to become unavoidable.

Meeting a higher standard

Leaders are facing an environment in which every one of their stakeholders has greater demands and higher expectations. Consumers increasingly want to buy from companies that reflect their values, they are starting to think twice about those with a negative environmental footprint (consider how supermarkets have scrambled to respond to criticism over excessive use of plastic in packaging), and they have new concerns such as how their online data is being used and stored. Employees similarly want to work for businesses they believe in (especially millennials, with numerous surveys showing many would take a pay cut in return for a better working environment, or to work for a company that matches their values). Investors want to know not just that your company has good commercial prospects, but that it meets their standards of diversity, environmental benefit and data protection.

Business cannot fall back on the old social contract: that it exists to provide jobs to its employees, products or services to its customers, and that those things alone should be enough. It has to understand that new expectations demand a refreshed contract: a moral bond through which employees are not just paid but nurtured and supported, and have their views represented; customers are not just serviced at the minimum level, but have their needs met and their interests protected; environmental impact is not an afterthought but something actively considered in all key decisions; and regulation is seen as a serious framework to be respected rather than something to be gamed and pushed to its limits.

The bottom line is no longer enough, in every part of your business. It's no longer enough to have a bottom-line relationship with your employees or customers, where loyalty is expected as the price of offering a job or providing a service in the first place. You can't have a bottom-line relationship with your suppliers and partners, where your economic needs are relentlessly pursued over theirs. And you can't have a bottom-line relationship with the ecosystem on which your business depends, minimising the amount of tax you spend while maximising the resources you take out. Employees can no longer be thought of as people who just work for you; customers as people who are only interesting because they buy from you; and society as something that only happens at the weekend.

Where CEOs have traditionally focused on the fiduciary duty to shareholders above all else, now the range of responsibilities has widened. Of course companies have always been responsible to their customers, employees and wider communities on some level, but never have those demands been so pressing or carried such immediate business consequences. Customers can be in direct touch with you or rant about you on social media; employees are rating your performance and behaviour for the world to see on Glassdoor; investors may withdraw funding based on a broader range of compliance and hygiene issues than was the case before.

From a prevailing model of business that was too tilted in favour of one interest group, the challenge has become how you hold many different interests and demands in balance. As a leader it is your responsibility to ensure that your company meets the higher standards that are being set, without losing focus on the essentials of your business model: because if you aren't creating value and making a profit, suddenly you won't be supporting any jobs or creating any positive social impact at all.

There are a number of organisations and frameworks that can help companies to meet their full range of responsibilities. The B Corp movement, of which Simply Business is a part, offers a framework for helping businesses improve their social and environmental impact, employee engagement, and transparency to the public. To become a B Corp you have to go through a rigorous assessment process, one that encourages you to think about the impact of your business in a holistic way, and to think about constant improvement. The Blueprint for Better Business is a charity which works with companies including the likes of Unilever and Vodafone to help them broaden and enhance their impact. It outlines five principles of purpose-driven business: purpose which delivers long-term sustainable performance; honesty and fairness with customers and suppliers; being a 'good citizen' (paying your taxes, helping the less privileged, being more conscious about stakeholders); being a 'responsible and responsive' employer; and a 'guardian for future generations'.

As frameworks rather than prescriptive templates, both organisations rightly reflect that the realities are different for every business. Depending on your size, sector, the nature of your workforce and the needs of your customers, the ways in which a company can meet these higher standards might vary significantly. That said, a universal factor is a company leadership that accepts the reality of increased responsibilities and which also plays a central role in helping to meet them.

In this context a good leader is also a custodian, taking decisions that are in the long-term business interest, and preventing ones that would damage its reputation or the interests of key stakeholders. You always have to be thinking: will the decision you are about to make support what customers need from you, what employees and investors expect from you, and what regulators demand of you? Are you being as transparent as you could be with customers? Are you looking after their data? Are you fulfilling your company mission and values? Are you being environmentally sound? A more complex set of priorities means decisions cannot just be made based on what is best for the bottom line; they also need to be stress-tested against what people want and expect from you as a business. And it is leaders who have both the perspective and the authority to keep all these factors and considerations in balance.

So how do you set about ensuring that you meet all these responsibilities as a leader, and navigate the volatile environment that every business now faces? It's a combination of several things: having a proper understanding of your mandate as a leader and where that authority comes from; how you represent your company in the public arena; and how you resist the pressures to compromise your values.

i) Represent: be the public face of your firm

Should a CEO be on the frontline of their business in external dealings or is it safer to keep to the comfort of the corner office? As expectations on companies increase and business becomes increasingly politicised, it is getting harder to hide away.

Most obviously, as a leader you are now more accessible than ever to your customers, and that is something you have to embrace. If I get an email from a customer, which probably happens around once a week, it will be the first thing to which I give my attention. If someone has taken the time to find my contact details and write to me, then it almost always means there has been a failure of our systems, products or customer service on some level. Not only do we need to fix the problem, we need to show the customer that we take it as seriously as they do. You cannot go and talk about putting customers first if you're not prepared to back it up, and that starts with leaders. A swift, direct and personal response is what's required.

The way leaders now have to represent their firms isn't limited to when problems arise, or even to issues directly relating to the business itself. We are also starting to see companies and their leaders speak out on broader issues and become more politically engaged. This growing strain of CEO activism has started to become noticeable in the last two to three years, especially since Donald Trump's election as US President. In that time, big brands have lined up in opposition against policies that include withdrawal from the Paris climate change agreement, a clampdown on undocumented migrants who arrived in the US as children (Dreamers), and the notorious travel ban on some Muslim-majority countries. In response to that, Starbucks CEO Howard Schulz announced that the company was pledging to hire 10,000 refugees. When the repeal of legislation allowing Dreamers the right to remain was announced, Microsoft President Brad Smith responded by saying that if the government attempted to deport a Microsoft employee, 'it's going to have to go through us to get to that person'. Much of that onus came from employees, with petitions signed at companies including IBM and Oracle urging the CEO to speak out.

In the view of Marc Benioff, CEO of the cloud computing giant Salesforce and often identified as one of the ringleaders of this emerging movement, 'Traditionally we've relied on our government leaders to express the values of our country and to fight for what's right. And I think now, the onus is more on CEOs.'

While activism is coming easily to some business leaders, others are still showing signs of reluctance when it comes to fronting up in public. Mark Zuckerberg's Congress hearing took place after several failed attempts to get him to appear, instead, lawyers and other company representatives were sent. Meanwhile, despite social media having become one of the main channels through which consumers can communicate with companies, a 2017 analysis showed that big company CEOs are generally staying away, with only 25 having an active Twitter account, and 60 per cent having no account on any of the major platforms.

When it comes to representing your business at more than annual meetings and pre-arranged press calls, some of the new expectations can clash with traditional inhibitions about exposing a business to either criticism or liability. 'Our lawyers said it was a terrible idea for me to tweet, but I ignored them, T-Mobile CEO John Legere, who now has a following of over 4.5 million on the platform, has said. 'This is no game. It's a way of driving my business. Much of what I do online is listen to customers, and social media is perfect for that.'

Leaders have to recognise that people increasingly want to be associated with companies that reflect their values, and that it is their responsibility to find ways of reflecting and representing those values in the public sphere. That doesn't mean you absolutely have to be on social media or wade in on every single debate. But you should be closely attuned to the mood of your employees, customers and investors, looking at issues on which they may expect you to express an opinion and represent their views. Leaders, who have often feared the consequences of being overexposed, need to understand that there is increasingly a price to pay for holding back and staying silent.

ii) Resist: don't compromise on your values

Faced with the need to meet higher standards of ethics and behaviour to earn public trust, companies need both a means to express what they believe and organise how they will behave. These values help people within the business to make decisions that underpin those beliefs rather than undermining them, and they can also be part of your relationship with customers, setting out what you commit to deliver to them.

There are some that roll their eyes when you talk about values, which can be generic and often sound the same across the board, regardless of what the business actually does. But when a company works hard to identify values that are both relevant and actually represent what it is trying to achieve, they become an essential tool for helping ensure a business has the ambition and also the capacity to meet higher expectations. So when we talk at Simply Business about empowerment, it means our people have the freedom to do things they think are important without having to get approval first, whether that is to do an experiment under their own steam or to send a gift or card to a customer who has had a difficult time. And when we emphasise learning as a core value, it's something we seek to embed through 'pair programming', where we team people up virtually across our UK and US offices to write software collaboratively and learn from each other.

But it's not just about what you do on an everyday basis to ensure your values are relevant as well as lived. As a leader trying to build a business based on strong values, there are going to be times when those come into conflict with the financial interest of the business. These moments provide the acid test decisions that show your team, investors and customers how serious you really are about the things you like to talk about.

One of the things our company prides itself on is providing insurance that actually works, meaning we are there for our customers when crisis hits and they need us most, helping them to get back on their feet. This was tested during the London Riots of 2011, when a group of our customers got caught up in the collateral damage, and we received a group of claims on the same day. The normal procedure would have been to send a claims assessor to assess the damage and make a recommendation before we paid out on anything. But I knew that to do this, and delay compensation, would add to the already significant distress people had suffered, and undermine our promise to be a true safety net for the businesses we insure. So I decided we would pay out on the claims in full on the same day, overriding the standard protocol.

As it turned out, two of the claims we received on that day were fraudulent, relating to damage that hadn't actually occurred. So we lost money by paying out to those who would have been shown on closer inspection to be trying it on. Even so, I never regretted making that decision, because if we had prevaricated, we would have lost credibility not just with our customers but within the business. At moments like that a team is looking to you to see which way you are going to jump, and what your priorities really are. This was relatively early in my tenure, and people later told me that was one of the moments when they started to believe we were actually going to build the kind of business we had been talking about, one that went out of its way to help customers when they really needed it.

Sometimes the audience for these decisions stretches well beyond your own team and the customers affected. When Delta Air Lines decided to cut ties with the National Rifle Association in the wake of the Parkland school shooting in March 2018, cancelling a discount partnership, the conservative state legislature in Georgia signalled its displeasure by rescinding a fuel tax break worth $40m to Delta. Its

CEO, Ed Bastian, was commendably robust in his response: 'Our decision was not made for economic gain and our values are not for sale,' he wrote in a letter to employees.

Although such decisions might mean an immediate loss of income, the potential cost of compromising on your values can be much greater; it could lose you customers or undermine the confidence and trust of your team. When people have come to work for you or done business with you based on the kind of business you are and what you believe, there is a price to pay for undermining those understandings, and eroding the basis on which they have made a choice to put their faith in you.

My early experience at Simply Business showed me that there is a cost to doing business with people who don't share your values or believe in what you are trying to achieve. The investors I inherited on arrival were individuals with no shared goal other than their own benefit and who fought against any moves that threatened to dilute that. I especially remember trying to push through an early pay rise for our contact centre team. We were talking about a financial commitment that was not onerous for the business and which had the potential to make a significant difference to employee satisfaction in an area of the business that has high staff turnover by default. Despite all that, and even though I knew that one of the directors had recently taken a personal loan from the business in excess of the amount we were discussing, it was a tough battle to get it through. It reinforced to me that it's very hard to have a serious conversation with the wrong investors about how to build a business that engenders loyalty and builds long-term value. You need to pick people who understand and support what you are trying to do, even if they won't necessarily always agree with how you do it.

One of the things I say to entrepreneurs starting out is that you generally have a lot more choice around raising capital than you think. When I was younger, I would just chase the deal and worry about the relationships afterwards, and I have had to learn from experience what a foolhardy approach that is. Instead, you should focus on picking partners who will be in it for the long haul: those who understand not only your industry and markets, but also what exactly you are trying to do and how you intend to do it. It's a lot easier than it once was. Two or three decades ago, I wouldn't have fancied trying to raise money given my background and the way I speak and come across. But the old boys club is not what it was, and ideas about responsible business, triple bottom line and social value are far less likely to be laughed out of pitch meetings than they would once have been.

Now there are patient capital funds, impact investors and ethical investment houses that are broadening the focus of a capital pool which is also becoming deeper. And there are investors with northern accents who didn't go to 'proper' universities. My advice is don't take money from people who have fundamentally different values from you. It is always going to lead to tension, something investors will often seek to resolve by dispensing with your services and finding someone more willing to serve their needs. One private equity backer, who I clashed with over budgets and targets, at one stage had a headhunter working to replace me, something I sensed at the time but only found out about later. I can't really blame him: after that meeting I started my own search to replace them, too.

If you have a vision and a values system for your business, then you need to find investors who at least understand and respect it, even if they don't always agree with it. Disagreements and creative tension are going to happen, and often they are beneficial, but that has to happen within some basic boundaries of agreement about what you are trying to achieve. Most of all, it should never get personal and it absolutely should never include an investor asking if you, and I quote, 'have the balls for the challenge'.

With those experiences in mind, I became more careful over time about who we partnered with, and especially mindful that there should always be a culture and values fit as well as the right financial offer. This was especially true when it came to our eventual acquisition by Travelers, the US insurance group. During this negotiation, one of the things I was most keen to establish was that shared values and under-standings existed that would allow our teams to work effectively together. I knew I could only recommend a deal to our team with credibility if I was sure that there was a cultural fit as well as a corporate one.

I particularly remember a meeting I set up during the diligence process between our respective heads of information security. Wayne, who normally looks and dresses like the younger sibling of Mick Jagger or Noel Fielding, asked me if he should break with habit and wear a suit to the meeting with his more obviously corporate counterpart. That was the last thing I wanted him to do, because the important thing was to see how our culture would collide with Travelers, as a listed company that employs over 30,000 people compared to our 500. As it was, the meeting went brilliantly, there was a great exchange of ideas and it helped convince me we could align two cultures that outwardly looked different but proved to have plenty in common, especially around valuing people. With that in mind, when I went to present the deal to the wider team I had confidence that it was something that people would get behind.

The important thing was to understand where my mandate to make that decision and conduct that negotiation came from. In a situation like that, I don't believe a leader is just negotiating in the financial interest of their business; they are also responsible for ensuring that the deal will uphold the interests and beliefs of employees and customers. Even when you are in a conversation about the financial future of your business, you cannot let your other responsibilities fall by the wayside. You have to remember in whose interests you are acting and what they expect of you. If you don't practise as a leader what you have been preaching all along, then everyone from your customers to your team is going to start losing faith in what you have to say, fatally undermining your attempts to build trust.

★★★

With companies under greater scrutiny and being asked to meet more responsibilities than before, the remit of leaders has become broader in turn. When there are so many different factors at work, it is the leader's job to hold together all the different threads and ensure that their business is meeting the needs of all its stakeholders, all of the time. You have to be the one questioning whether a particular decision has taken into account all the many factors now surrounding a business, seeing ahead to potential risk factors and vulnerabilities, and standing firm when your values or mission as a business might be at risk of being compromised.

That means as a leader you have to both personally embody the values of your company and also act as the ultimate guardian of them. It is no good talking about being democratic, for instance, if you insist on making all the decisions; about being straightforward and transparent, but having a terms of business document that needs a lawyer to translate it; or about having a flat hierarchy one minute and closing the door on your corner office the next.

You also need to have a keen sense of where your mandate and authority to lead come from. Once this was vested in the role and status of being a CEO or senior manager. Traditional, more hierarchical organisations enshrined the idea that the boss's word is law. J. Edgar Hoover, the notoriously dictatorial FBI director for almost 50 years, once responded to a memo with the message: 'Watch the borders'. Agents were duly put into action on the Mexican and Canadian borders; in fact Hoover had been complaining that not enough space had been left on the margins of the document.

You will not get very far today by hoping that people respect your decisions just because you are the one making them. Your authority as a leader arises much more from how you do your job than the fact that you happen to hold it. You are being judged in everything you do by employees, customers and investors; they are looking at how you act and behave, not just the results you achieve.

All these things are fundamentally about how you build trust, which has always been one of the most important jobs for any leader. What has changed is that trust has become harder to win, quicker to lose and it needs to be sought from many more people. It is no longer just about getting people to trust that you are a capable manager who will steer the ship in a profitable and stable way. People also need to believe that your intentions and impact are good, there are no skeletons in your cupboard (be that a yawning pay-gap, a non-diverse management team, a question-able tax record, poor pay or treatment of workers), and that you will be as good as your word and live up to your values.

The decline in trust in business is a long-term trend, and linked to that in institutions as a whole. The only way to slowly reverse it is through enough businesses showing that they can meet a broader range of responsibilities, beyond the traditional economic ties between company and customer, employer and employee. Which means that top of any leader's agenda there need to be three essential questions that you ask yourself at all times: What are our responsibilities as a business in their entirety? Who do we owe them to? And what are we going to do to meet them?

PART IV

Rebooting work

'In economic terms, we've gone from an Industrial Economy – where we hired hands – to a Knowledge Economy – where we hired heads – to what is now a Global Human Economy – where we hire hearts.'

Dov Seidman
Author of *How* and CEO of LRN

CHAPTER 8

HAPPY AND HUMAN

'What will happen, then, to the men in today's jobs? Can we all live on the wealth of automatic factories and the earnings of an elite band of 60,000 software engineers?

'It's time to think about the future.'

A timely thought, impressively so given that it was voiced 40 years before this book was written. In 1978, a *Horizon* documentary explored the impact of microprocessors on traditional industry, and what the effects on employment might be.

'In the long term, when the only plentiful resource is going to be people, is automation the wrong road to take?' it pondered. 'Could this technology be the end of an age, the end of a line of evolution and not a beginning? But in the short term, can we afford not to automate?'

The same questions are now being asked again as the capabilities of artificial intelligence and machine learning increase, and the implications for the working world start to become clear. Thirty-five years after that programme broadcast, two Oxford University engineering academics published a paper with a seemingly unremarkable question: 'How susceptible are jobs to computerisation?' Their 45-page article was distilled into a single headline that went around the world: 47 per cent of American jobs at high risk of automation in the next two decades. It lit the fuse on a debate about the future of work in a world dominated by technology, and the predictions have hardly stopped coming since. In the UK, the Bank of England has put the number of jobs threatened by automation at 15 million. A more recent OECD study was more sanguine, estimating that only 14 per cent of jobs across its 35 member nations were at high risk of automation, though that still totals 66 million.

As these analyses have poured out, the way we work now, and what it will look like in the future, has become one of the major debating topics in the business world. People's rising disenchantment with their work, if a number of large-scale studies are to be believed, coupled with anxiety over what the effects of automation and ubiquitous AI will be on jobs, mean there is both an unhappy present and an uncertain future to navigate.

There is a tendency for the debate about work to focus on the future half of this equation, looking at which jobs are going to be automated and when, and what the worst-case scenarios might be. Important as that may be, there are also problems right now that demand attention and new ideas. The reboot in work that is required needs to address both sides of this question: how we tackle the shortcomings of the status quo and how we can prepare people for what the jobs of the future may be like. We need to think about how people can be happier and more fulfilled in their working lives, and what the role of human intelligence and skills is going to look like in a world increasingly dominated by machines. This is a challenge companies need to grasp, because as I've already discussed, the single greatest component in any successful business is a team of happy, motivated people.

Our current working model, one that has left so many people around the world feeling disengaged from their work at the same time as being stressed by its demands and unproductive in its delivery, is a curious mixture: old habits and practices that have lingered well past their sell-by date alongside new tools that we probably don't use as effectively as we should.

Rebooting this working model will involve unpicking some of the understandings that underpin it, which date back to the management theory and working practices of the early 20th century. It demands a different approach to how people are managed, one that ensures greater autonomy; a rethink about how employees should be motivated, moving beyond the limitations of financial incentives; a more deliberate relationship with the technology we already use in our work today; and preparation for the working world that the next wave of technology is going to create.

Creating autonomy

'It is only through *enforced* standardisation of methods, *enforced* adoption of the best implements and working conditions, and *enforced* cooperation that […] faster work can be assured. And the duty of enforcing the adoption of standards and enforcing this cooperation rests with *management* alone.' So decreed Frederick Taylor, the original management theorist, writing in 1911. His guiding idea was 'scientific management': maximising productivity through the establishment of measurable targets, training people for specific roles and putting them into repeatable systems that eliminated inefficiency as far as possible.

If his goal was efficiency, his enemy was what he called 'systematic soldering', the practice of deliberately working below capacity to maximise the number of people that were required. Taylor's method was standardisation, prescribing a set technique for everything from how bricks were laid to how cars were assembled, ideas he developed through time and motion studies he conducted with the aid of a stopwatch. In other words, he was the father of micro-management, an ethos grounded in a fundamental mistrust of the people whose output you are trying to maximise.

Though Taylor's ideas had many critics, their influence has been long lasting. If I think back to my call centre experience, it was an environment of which he would almost certainly have approved. We worked 8 hours a day, 20 minutes for lunch, with a red light constantly flashing on the handset and a screen in our line of vision showing how many calls were waiting. I was lucky: we were well paid and, given we were expected to have good knowledge about the destinations we were selling, there was plenty of opportunity to go abroad. Still, there was no getting away from the relentlessness of the job and the total lack of personal freedom. It wasn't just the demands of incoming calls that kept us glued to our phones; if you fell below the 70 per cent of the working day mandated to be spent at your desk available for a call, your manager would issue you with a warning. When I was duly called in and made the point that I could try to be at my desk more but thought my productivity and output would probably fall as a result, it fell on deaf ears. That was the rule, and the rule was all that mattered.

If you approached the average CEO today and asked them if they'd like to run their company on the lines of a factory from the 1900s, then you can imagine the response you'd get. But far too many companies still do operate along those lines philo-sophically, even as the structures and work environments superficially evolve. The spirit of Taylor – that people are units to be organised as efficiently and productively as possible – is still alive and well in large parts of the collective business culture. Some have even argued that, with the tools now available to track in real time every movement and output of individual workers, there is a new form of digitally driven Taylorism emerging, especially prevalent in the warehouse environments of large retailers.

If we are to reverse people's disengagement from work and unhappiness with it, there is a need not just to do away with the remnants of Taylorism in practice, but to throw out the world view that underpinned the method. Where scientific management was about a lack of trust in people and minimising the scope for any kind of autonomy, the modern context calls for an approach which both trusts and empowers people in their work, giving them more freedom to work how, when and where they want to.

Autonomy, the antithesis of Taylorism, is what most employees now actively seek. An experiment run by researchers at the University of Cologne found that people were two and a half times more likely to want to swap a job of influence and power for one with autonomy than vice versa. Gallup's 2017 survey of the US workforce found that 54 per cent of American office workers would change jobs if it gave them the option to work flexibly. Employees who are given more freedom in their work have also been shown to have higher levels of job satisfaction and wellbeing, according to a study of more than 20,000 workers by University of Birmingham academics.

The most obvious freedom, one that is now offered by around half of UK and American employers, is flexible working arrangements. That is something we do at Simply Business, in our head office, where people can work in whatever way suits them, and in our contact centre, where we recently got rid of desktop phones and equipped people with laptops and headsets to take customer calls anywhere in the office or, if they prefer, at home.

But although flexible working is an important starting point, and something that is definitely on the rise, giving people autonomy is about more than when and where they work. It's also about a deeper sense that people have the power to shape their own working life and career path, and that they are working in a trusting environment rather than one which seeks to monitor and assess them at every turn. It's about being able to work on things you are interested in, in a way that suits you, without needless restrictions on your personal freedoms and endless hoops to jump through.

That is why we have slimmed down the targets we measure our contact-centre teams against from more than 20 when I arrived to only a handful, focusing on the quality of conversations rather than the volume. We want to help people do the one thing that matters most, which is have friendly and helpful conversations with customers, rather than have them focused on filling an hourly or daily quota of calls. Instead of holding people to quantitative targets, we now do more in the way of qualitative feedback based on a consultant's ability to interact with the customer and overall compliance. This seeks to be more of a coaching-style relationship than the teacher-pupil dynamic that target numbers enshrine. Similarly, with our head-office team we don't carry out annual appraisals, and individual project teams will decide if and how to set specific objectives and targets against which to measure success.

Autonomy is also about where you allow ideas to come from, and giving people the freedom to help shape their own working environment and conditions. One of the most important changes we made in our contact centre was as a direct result of a suggestion that came from within the team. This was a shift from specialised teams who dealt with sales, customer service and renewals. At one of our hackathons, someone suggested that we should break down the silos and have all our customer consultants working across all of these areas. The idea was that having our consultants work across every aspect of our customer relationships would encourage better empathy for different needs and ultimately support stronger relationships. It was also about trying to break from a system which encouraged those who worked in sales to focus on conversions and nothing else. So we ran it as an experiment and it worked: customer metrics went up, so did employee NPS, and we have since rolled it out across the whole contact centre. Along with the shift to a more flexible working arrangement, it has been one of the best changes to working practices we have made.

And it was all the better for being an idea that was championed from within rather than imposed or suggested from above.

Not every change in our working practices has been so seamless, and I haven't always been as receptive to ideas from within the team as I should have been. While we now operate a fully flexible working arrangement with our head-office team, it wasn't always the case. When the idea was first proposed we were a couple of years into what had been a sustained, concerted effort to build a meaningful culture, and on every key business metric, from customer and revenue growth to employee retention, it was working. I didn't like the idea of opening the door to remote working – not because I didn't trust that people would continue to do their jobs properly, but because I worried about the impact it would have on the culture and sense of togetherness that we had created. Would we not dilute that very special ethos that had been such an important factor in our nascent success?

In fact, so strong was my objection that I went against one of the principles I have outlined in this book, and overruled the results of the first experiment that had been undertaken, by two of our most senior software developers on their own initiative. The test was done, the results came back – people worked productively, continued to collaborate and enjoyed the flexibility – and it should have been all systems go. However, I was convinced there was something intangible that the data wouldn't and couldn't tell us. That some part of the essential mix would be lost by letting people scatter to the four winds. So I shut it down and declared we would carry on as before.

It was only after about a month that it fully dawned on me how counter-cultural, and therefore mistaken, that decision had been. My view on the issue was so strong that I had allowed it to override one of the basic tenets of the business, which is that we are led by data not biases, and informed by experiments and not assumptions. So I made a better decision, and encouraged the team to do another, longer, experiment, looking at the relationship between flexible working and our culture. This ran for around three months, and it effectively determined its own conclusions: that remote working was something people enjoyed, was productive for the business and which didn't damage either the culture or people's ability to work effectively together. In some form that experiment is still going three years later. We reached a point – more by natural development than any grand decision – that individual teams and project groups should determine their own way of working, and decide what operating rhythm suits them best. And that is exactly as it should be, people directing and setting the terms of their own working pattern according to what is best for them and their colleagues.

There are perhaps limits to how far autonomy can take you towards a more productive and empowering work environment. At the extreme, companies like Zappos have pursued a so-called holacracy, where you essentially do away with centralised management and people and teams organise themselves. The idea, Zappos founder Tony Hsieh has said, was for the company 'to function more like a city and less like a top-down bureaucratic organisation.' Cities become more productive the larger they grow but companies do not, he reasoned. In practice holacracy has meant as much confusion and extra bureaucracy (with the codifying of roles and responsibilities for each project) as it has freedom and empowerment. Julia Culen, a management consultant who worked under the system for a year, has written that 'Holacracy … was designed by engineers and that is what it felt like, once I was in it. I felt like being part of a code, operating [within] an algorithm that is optimised for machines, but not for humans. Instead of feeling more whole, self-organised and more powerful, I felt trapped.'

Medium, the online publishing platform, was another of the companies to experiment with the system, but ultimately abandoned it, with its then head of operations writing that it was 'difficult to co-ordinate efforts at scale'. Zappos itself has seen struggles with the system, with a 29 per cent staff turnover in one year after fully implementing the system; it also fell out of the *Fortune* list of the best American companies to work for in 2016, having featured for the previous seven years.

Ultimately most people do want some form of structure, even if that should be far less prescriptive than those we have derived from Taylor's scientific management model. You need to give people clarity over what they are meant to be doing and feedback they can use, within a framework that allows for a healthy degree of self-direction, whether that is over small issues (like where to work) or large ones (what to work on). A rebooted model of work will be one in which both people and companies feel the benefit of greater autonomy, higher trust and the improved performance that follows.

Changing incentives

If a move towards greater autonomy is one way in which we can improve work today, another is to rethink how people are incentivised. Traditional financial motivations, especially the annual bonus round, are another of our inheritances from the worldview of Taylor. In his treatise on scientific management he outlined the 'initiative and incentive' system: 'in order to have any hope of obtaining the initiative of his workmen the manager must give some special incentive to his men beyond that which is given to the average of the trade,' he wrote, listing financial bonuses among other incentives that included the promise of promotion, better working conditions and shorter hours. The essential idea that people are motivated by financial self-interest above all has been one of Taylorism's most pervasive legacies.

Our understanding of this question has been significantly enhanced in the last decade by advances in behavioural economics: the study of how we make decisions and what influences us as we do so. Although its roots stretch back to the 1940s, and the Hungarian mathematician John von Neumann's articulation of game theory, it was not until a decade ago that behavioural economics entered the mainstream as a lens for understanding how people interpret choices and make decisions. A tipping point was the publication of the book *Nudge* by Richard Thaler and Cass Sunstein, which demonstrated how changing people's 'choice environment' – in as simple a way as altering the default option or the phrasing of a question on a form – can radically alter how people make decisions and can be steered towards certain choices.

Behavioural economics has been eagerly adopted by governments worldwide, for purposes from securing prompt tax payments to encouraging organ donation via an opt-out system rather than opt-in. In 2017, the rise of behavioural economics was confirmed when Richard Thaler was awarded the Nobel Prize for economics, following in the footsteps of Daniel Kahneman 15 years earlier. Thaler's work has been central to dismantling the prevailing wisdom that people are fundamentally logical and rational thinkers, who weigh evidence to make decisions in their own interest.

The moment a behavioural economics lens is applied to traditional management thinking, many of the assumptions supporting traditional performance incentives start to fall apart. As the behavioural expert Daniel Pink, author of *Drive*, has argued, 'there is a mismatch between what science knows and what business does.' While we increasingly, at least in theory, understand the importance of what Pink terms intrinsic motivators ('the desire to do things because they matter, because we like it, they're interesting, or part of something important'), business is still focused on the extrinsic, and financial motivators.

Criticism of this approach has increased in recent years. Not only have some studies shown that people generally respond better to intrinsic motivators, such as opportunity to do more interesting work, than to extra money, but some researchers have argued that misapplied financial incentives can actually demotivate people: 'Financial incentives may [...] reduce intrinsic motivation and diminish ethical or other reasons for complying with workplace social norms such as fairness,' the LSE's Dr Bernd Irlenbusch has said. 'As a consequence, the provision of incentives can result in a negative impact on overall performance.' This was something tested by Duke University behavioural economist Dan Ariely, who ran an experiment with employees at Intel's semiconductor factory. Targets were set, with different groups offered a different reward for meeting them: a cash bonus, pizza voucher, note of thanks from their boss and no reward at all. Those in the cash reward group were 13 per cent less productive than those in the no-reward group, while the other two incentives saw high productivity for a number of days afterwards.

This is not new news. Twenty-five years ago, the social scientist Alfie Kohn was writing in the *Harvard Business Review* that, 'by and large, rewards succeed at securing one thing only: temporary compliance. When it comes to producing lasting change in attitudes and behaviour, however, rewards, like punishment, are strikingly ineffective. Once the rewards run out, people revert to their old behaviours.' And yet despite the growing body of evidence that bonuses aren't that effective at encouraging performance, they are still pervasive across business. The ONS has calculated that £46.4bn was paid out in bonuses to UK employees in the year ending March 2017, the highest ever figure.

My experience is that bonuses can do more to create difficulties than they do to spread goodwill and motivate people. The annual giveaway, if you choose to have one, is riddled with psychological potholes. Those who receive a good bonus may merely feel that they are getting what they deserved; those who don't, or receive an amount below what they were after, are going to feel badly treated. By definition, you are setting expectations high, and likely to generate only neutrality or disappointment as a result. There's not much trust in an environment where the employer holds back some of the money and makes it contingent on whether they judge you to have done the job well or not. People don't trust that they are being given what they deserve, even if they do get a bonus. And they wonder if the person next to them is getting a better deal, and if that is down to anything more than individual relationships.

When I started at Simply Business I made it very clear that in year 1 there would be no bonuses. Instead we raised salaries by an equivalent amount; far better, in my view, to give people the money they are owed, rather than to make it contingent on a series of factors that are meant to be objective but which often come down to whether a particular line manager likes you or not. In the contact centre we have also been getting rid of target-linked bonuses and giving the money to people on an unconditional basis. In place of individual performance bonuses, we have a straightforward profit-sharing scheme, similar to that of John Lewis, based on us hitting our financial metrics. We track this quarterly so everyone has a sense of where we are and what they are in line to get.

Most importantly of all, we have an equity share scheme, which means our whole team has a stake in our long-term success. This is one of the things I am most proud of: when I first suggested it to our then private equity partner, they said it was against their policy to distribute equity beyond the management team. So we devised our own scheme, redistributing a portion of the management's equity to our entire team. Even though it meant some people giving up a not insignificant portion of personal income, it was voted through by the management without question. Doing so meant everyone saw a dividend when we sold the business, which ended up happening twice in the course of six months (first to a new private equity partner and then Travelers). It is this money that people often say has helped to fund life ambitions, from becoming a property owner to going on dream holidays.

There is a collective benefit too to a system like this, which helps to foster a sense of common ownership right across the business. A business of many owners has a collective level of engagement and responsibility that is quite different from those where equity is concentrated in a few hands. Along with greater autonomy, it is part of creating an ownership mindset where people have more control over their working lives and get to share in the proceeds of growth. It is about motivating people through what they can achieve, rather than having a reductive focus on targets and bonuses that assumes people come to work every day thinking about what they will get at the end of the year. Or to put it another way, it's about treating people as people and accepting the complexity of what motivates us, rather than units of production whose output can be optimised with a twist of the bonus dial.

Rethinking our use of technology

It is not just overly prescriptive management systems, and an outmoded notion of what motivates people, that have made the status-quo model of work increasingly unsuited to people's needs. The way we use technology in the workplace is another factor that is contributing to the malaise, and it is one which demands a new and more deliberate approach.

Technology that has entirely changed how we communicate, from email to smartphones, has actually worked in the opposite way from how most imagined, and added to most workloads. People feel less able than ever to fully separate themselves from work, even at weekends and on holiday. And it affects how people behave and work together in the office. Instant messenger services are becoming commonplace, even though one study suggested that face-to-face communication is 34 times more effective when asking someone to do something. Meetings can be a parade of laptops and smartphones as much as a focused discussion on the matter at hand. The problem isn't that this technology exists, but that we haven't thought enough about how we use it and what effect that has on people's ability to be productive, switch off from work at weekends and on holiday, and to work together effectively.

It was my experience using Google Glass, the much-hyped but short-lived (in its initial incarnation) attempt to let us wear the Internet as a pair of glasses, that helped me come round to this view. The principle might have been a good one. But there is no substitute for looking like a total prat to make you stop and think about whether something (in this case ubiquitous technology) is actually a good idea or not. Although I was enthusiastic to start with, as soon as I tried them on, I realised I didn't want emails popping up in my peripheral vision. I didn't want to be distracted when meeting someone for the first time by having a load of information about them appear as some kind of one-way wall between us. And I didn't like the fact they made me look stupid.

My experiment lasted for just one morning, but it had one longer lasting effect, which was to make me start thinking seriously about something I had been toying with for some time: whether our use of technology was becoming too much of a good thing, and what to do about it within the business.

On this issue I had a bit of the zeal of the convert, having picked up bad habits in my previous job and become a pretty full-on phone addict myself. What I knew from the experience is that you don't notice your own behaviour, and how technology affects it. It was only when our COO gave me a pep talk that it started to sink in. Do you realise, he said, that the moment someone loses your attention in a meeting, you pull out your phone and start doing emails? I didn't, and that in itself was part of the problem. Our relationships with personal technology have become so instinctive, so compulsive that we hardly even notice ourselves slipping out of the room we are sitting in and into the virtual world that's constantly buzzing away in our pockets.

We now know that our phone fixation is no accident; the apps that keep us pushing and swiping all day long have been designed to keep us glued, rewarding us with notifications and interactions that deliver dopamine shots to the brain, a neurological cycle that stokes its own demand and keeps us coming back for more. As the technology entrepreneur Tristan Harris has suggested, apps and devices are being designed in the same way that food manufacturers use sugar and salt to encourage binge eating. App makers are now as much neuroscientists and behavioural psychologists as game designers. As Ramsay Brown, co-founder of the appropriately named app consultancy Dopamine Labs, has said, companies 'need your eyeballs locked in that app as long as humanly possible [...] they're all in a technological arms race to keep you there the longest.' In his words, 'We're really living in this new era that we're not just designing software any more, we're designing minds.'

With personal technology having become so invasive and addictive, companies need to draw clearer boundaries about how their people make use of such technology, both to support productivity and encourage wellbeing. This has begun to happen, with some implementing measures to limit email traffic and stop people having to work when they are away from the office.

Atos, the French IT services company, was one of the first to sound the alarm about the productivity pitfalls of too much email. In 2011, CEO Thierry Breton announced the ambition to become a 'zero email' company within three years. 'We are producing data on a massive scale that is fast polluting our working environments and encroaching into our personal lives,' he said, likening email overload to the environmental pollution caused by the factories of the Industrial Revolution. Internal research showed the company's managers were spending between 5 and 20 hours a week reading or responding to emails. As well as training programmes on how to reduce the reliance on email, Atos created an internal platform to host discussion threads about individual topics and projects, one that crucially did not ping a notification to an employee when a new message arrived, and was accessed at the individual user's discretion. Atos did not become zero email but did manage to reduce traffic by around 60 per cent within the first three years. It also estimated a 25 per cent increase in available work time, and 30 per cent improvement in customer satisfaction.

Daimler, the German car maker, has extended the same principle to holiday time, with a policy where your emails are auto-deleted and people trying to contact you are invited to speak with someone else or to get back in touch when you return.

We have experimented and discussed similar measures at Simply Business. On holiday emails we give people the option to have them deleted, though some prefer to stay in touch, and we won't ban that. Not everyone has shown complete willingness to let holiday be holiday. 'You don't really delete your emails, do you?' was a message I once got from an investor who had received my standard out-of-office message, moments after I had put it on and was getting ready to leave the office (gist: I take email off my phone while on holiday, messages I receive while away will be deleted, but if you really need me, call me). 'You will be checking in?' he added.

Similarly, when we floated the idea of throttling email so it would only appear at certain times of day, helping create entirely email-free parts of the day that could allow people to concentrate without distraction, the consensus was that people would be more anxious about the messages they were missing than liberated, so we didn't go ahead. There is no one policy that will suit every company: you have to do what works in the context of your business, but it should be a deliberate decision based on what people want and what supports productivity, not the free-for-all that has been too common with technology in the workplace.

In one area we have been less permissive, however, and that is use of technology in meetings. When I arrived, meetings were one of the problem areas. People didn't listen, clearly switched off, and in one case I even saw someone who had visibly fallen asleep at the back of an all-hands update meeting, and someone else reading a book on the Kindle app on their phone. Which is far from ideal, albeit a useful ego check.

Even after the overall culture had started to improve, people who had a huge amount of mutual respect, and who wouldn't have dreamed of blanking each other in the office kitchen for example, would show no respect at all to the people presenting or leading meetings. Phones out, faces down.

I didn't mind about people being on their phones, in general. If someone wants to play Fruit Ninja five hours a day at their desk, then as long as they get their work done, they can go right ahead as far as I'm concerned (and they'd be in the company of prime ministers, if the stories about David Cameron are to be believed). But I was struck by the impact of phones on behaviour, especially in the relatively rare moments where we came together as a team to discuss the most important things we were working on. With so much psychological incentive baked into the technology, you are fighting a losing battle if you try to compete. Trying to run a productive meeting while people have full access to their smartphones is a bit like organising a quit-smoking clinic where you leave packets of cigarettes lying around the room. It has all the logical integrity of McDonald's' sponsorship of the Olympics. As Clay Shirky, the academic and networks expert who has written about banning technology in his lectures, concluded: 'The [tech] industry has committed itself to an arms race for my students' attention, and if it's me against Facebook and Apple, I lose.'

So we took a decision to get rid of technology from meetings. Not 'let's go easy' or 'please don't use your phone', but an outright ban. We would do meetings the old-fashioned way: person to person, notes with pen and paper if you wanted to, and no bottomless well of distraction tempting everyone away from the matter at hand. Only those leading the meeting, if they needed the aid of slides or similar, were allowed to use technology.

If that sounds like a school classroom, with me as the teacher telling people to put away their phones (which I did quite a lot to start with), there was one crucial difference: attendance became optional. No one has to attend a meeting they don't find interesting or useful. But if you are going attend, we now ask, then *really* attend. Have the courtesy to listen to the material that has often been carefully prepared, engage fully in the discussion, and take away what you need.

If that isn't going to help you, and you feel your time would be better spent doing some work, or playing a game at your desk, then do that instead.

The aim is not to control people's behaviour but to focus it, and to make everyone think about how their use of technology impacts on their ability to be productive, work effectively with others and enjoy a meaningful work-life balance.

The question of how to best deploy technology in the workplace goes beyond how people communicate and work together in meetings. It's also about new capabilities that technology is giving to companies, and what use (or not) they choose to make of them. For instance, one of the most obvious tools at the disposal of most companies is technology that allows you to track the activity of your employees: collecting data that will allow you to assess overall productivity and make decisions to improve working conditions or practices. This is what the *Telegraph* newspaper tried to do in 2016, with its journalists arriving at work one day to find black boxes had been attached to the undersides of their desks. After researching the brand name on the devices, it was quickly established that they were heat and motion sensors, designed to monitor the usage of a working area by how often someone was present (described by the provider with the not-at-all dystopian phrase of 'automated workplace utilisation analysis').

The jargon might be too long to fit on your average protest placard, but an outcry soon developed and the black boxes were first decried as Big Brother in action, and then swiftly removed. The people whose behaviour was being monitored quite reasonably believed that they were under surveillance, with their daily routine to be tracked, assessed, and quite possibly used as evidence against them. The *Telegraph* said that it was a data-gathering exercise to help them make better use of office space and boost energy efficiency; and that there had never been any intention to track activity back to individuals. Similar devices are apparently now becoming popular with other companies, especially banks looking to reduce the space they need to rent in expensive parts of the City.

The temptation is just to plug in technology like this wherever you can. Why not gather more information that will help you to make better decisions, for both employees and customers? Data science 101, right? Well it is, except this is an attitude that disregards the human element in any organisation. At one point, I considered a scheme where we would track the behaviour of our top-performing people, understand how they worked through a series of data points, and effectively try and create the model for how the best people go about their day job. I wanted to see if variables such as email usage, number of people in someone's network, office attendance, number of breaks, number of meetings and so on were positive indicators of success that other people could learn from. It sounded like a great idea, with plenty of utility, until I started to think about how I might feel if I was one of those people, having my every last movement and habit monitored. Viewed through that lens it was an obvious non-starter, and I'm glad it never went beyond an idle thought.

There are plenty of flaws in a mindset that looks to continuously integrate technology without sufficient care for how people will respond. The most significant is that it undermines the one thing that you need above all to build a resilient business in today's market, which is trust. As the story of the *Telegraph* and its sensors shows, when people have to fill in the gaps for themselves, they can easily end up with a much more dramatic conclusion than is probably warranted. What's more, even if a new development is properly introduced and explained, that doesn't mean people are going to like the idea that their working lives are more surrounded and scrutinised by technology than ever before.

We have been through enough cycles of technological change to know that there are almost always unintended consequences. Companies should be alive not just to the opportunities to achieve greater efficiency and productivity, but to the human realities of introducing new systems and tools, especially ones that seek to observe and influence people's behaviour. Just as driverless cars are having to navigate roads still dominated by human drivers, technology in business is something that has to work in harmony with people's needs and behaviour. And as much as the productivity benefits of technology matter, so too does the way it is perceived by the people who have to use it.

Finally, remember that technology is a tool and nothing more; an enabler and catalyst to help you change your business so it can do more and better for its customers. Technology is the means and not the end. And that, amid all the evangelism, mythologising and bold predictions, is the most important thing to keep in mind. It is still people who matter most. Technology should be seen as a tool in service of human needs, one that should be used to put people more in control of their working lives, in and out of the office.

Anticipating automation

At the same time as we seek to improve the way people work today, we also need to start thinking about the new world of work that technology will create. In particular that means addressing the fears that have emerged in recent years about automation, and its potential to cut a swathe through the labour market as artificial intelligence and machine learning reach into areas of work that existing technology has so far left untouched.

Are the robots really coming for us and our jobs? Schools of thought differ markedly over exactly how far technology will change work and how quickly. There is the dystopian future, where technology becomes all-powerful, renders jobs and human labour redundant, and ultimately decides it can do without its inventors after all. Game over for the humans and we become a footnote in an evolutionary story that goes beyond our species. Or there's the utopian version, where technology doesn't overpower humanity but merges with it, we upload our brains into the cloud and become positively superhuman, with radically enhanced cognitive and social functions. There's also the incremental version, where the pace of technological change and automation picks up, but doesn't fundamentally blow apart the status quo. And there's the downright cynical version, which points and laughs at our inability to get even the most basic technology working consistently, and asks, How do you really expect to go from faulty broadband connections to all-powerful, human-replacing robots in a generation?

I experienced that last one particularly vividly a few years ago, at the end of a week spent at the Singularity University (SU) in California, a rollercoaster ride through the potential of innovations from robotics through nanotechnology and genetic technology. Then, after a week of hearing about how dramatically emerging technologies were going to transform our world, we had a session lined up with Ray Kurzweil, SU founder and Google executive, on his vision of a singularity, the grand merger between human and machine intelligence (option 2). Except we had to wait 10 minutes, while a whole group of AV technicians struggled to get his presentation working. That's right: a piece of ambitious future gazing by one of the world's most admired tech thinkers, brought low by the most basic tech malfunction in the world. And if one of the world's leading experts on the future of technology can't get the IT working, what hope for the rest of us?

That experience didn't make me into one of the cynics, but I'm definitely closer to being an incrementalist than a utopian or dystopian. It's obvious to see the impact that artificial intelligence is already having in many business sectors: chatbots, which we use in our contact centre at Simply Business, and which have the potential to automate some aspects of customer service currently carried out by humans; algorithms that can replace human processing tasks, such as the reading and sorting of CVs in recruitment; and automated vehicles, which could reduce the need for truck drivers across the US and Europe by up to 70 per cent in the next decade.

However, while all of these developments – just a handful of the many examples of where artificial intelligence is already being applied – have the potential to be industry-changing, none are without their shortcomings. I can tell you from experience that chatbots, however much they might be talked up as the killer app for customer service, provide only a fraction of the functionality that you need to respond to the full range of customer needs that the average call centre will encounter. They can function as decision trees to move towards a fixed end point in a customer enquiry (like what kind of product would be most relevant), but their flexibility and ability to interact with people is still very basic. CV-reading software, while becoming more popular and in theory having the ability to both save recruiters time and address the problem of unconscious bias in hiring, can be gamed like any other algorithm (most obviously in this case through judicious use of keywords). And while a self-driving truck might perform brilliantly chugging down the motorway, it cannot repair itself in case of a breakdown, and will likely struggle with narrow local roads and the mechanics of the loading bay.

Indeed the auto industry as a whole, which has been trying to unlock the benefits of automation for decades, is a testament to the challenges that are involved in taking the power of artificial intelligence from concept to reality.

It was through automation that General Motors tried to arrest its decline in the early 1980s, under heavy pressure from Japanese car makers. CEO Roger Smith led an attempt to shift to 'lights out' manufacturing, automating large parts of the production line in an attempt to narrow the cost advantage of GM's Asian competitors and address increasingly acute reliability issues. But then the robots went rogue. Buick bumpers ended up on Cadillac chassis. Spray-painting robots started painting each other not the cars. Confusion reigned. As Paul Ingrassia and Joseph White relate in *Comeback,* their history of the American auto industry in the 1980s and 90s: 'GM's factory hands were stymied by the confusing array of robots and software. When a massive computer-controlled "robogate" welding machine smashed a car body, or a welding machine stopped dead, the entire [production] line would stop. Workers could do nothing but stand around and wait while managers called in the robot contractor's technicians.'

Fast forward to 2018 and Tesla, poster child for the future of transport, is reported to be facing not dissimilar problems. According to a leaked research report from investment analysts at Bernstein, Tesla's obsessive focus on automation has been leading them to spend twice as much as their competitors on manufacturing each unit. The relatively modest labour savings are being wiped out by the extensive capital costs of installing all the robotic technology. While an attempt to automate the final assembly stage is leading to poor manufacturing standards, with machines especially deficient in recognising mistakes and aligning the geometry of different components. 'The problem is automation is expensive – and usually proves far less effective, highly inflexible and creates quality problems further down the line,' the report concluded.

The GM and Tesla examples, spanning the best part of 40 years, show how big the gap really is between technology in principle and in practice. Just because automation is possible, and should in theory make things more efficient, reliant and lower-cost, doesn't mean it actually will in a given set of business circumstances.

New technology in theory is one thing; putting it into practice generally requires a lot more than plug and play. Systems and structures have to be adapted and often designed around the new technology; snagging factors and new challenges – in contemporary factories, a mechanised robot arm might be affected by anything from a software update

to a cyber attack – need to be managed; and significant investment almost certainly has to be made in
order to create the context and conditions in which
new technology can perform effectively. You need
to think and plan for how new technology is actually going to work with the people and processes
you have in place. As Ingrassia and White concluded
about GM's automation malfunctions: 'GM hadn't
reorganised work so that fewer people could do
it … They had simply grafted robots onto the old,
inefficient system.'

The potential of technologies such as robotics and
artificial intelligence is vast, but the application is
going to be gradual and problem-ridden, as has
always been the case with transformative technologies. History and experience tell us it is naive at best
to assume that technologies will be adopted and
deliver gains at the rate their creators and early
champions predict. They also tell us that focusing
on new technical capabilities in isolation is not the
way to draw effective conclusions or make efficient
progress.

As Bill Gates once said, long before automation
had become the major debating point it is now:
'The first rule of any technology used in a business
is that automation applied to an efficient operation
will magnify the efficiency. The second is that
automation applied to an inefficient operation will
magnify the inefficiency.'

At the moment, when it comes to AI, we are
essentially talking about algorithms that are in many

ways advanced and hugely powerful, but mainly functional when pointed towards specific, narrow-range problems that are rules and logic based. In the view of Berkeley computer science Professor Michael I. Jordan, 'What we will have is AI systems like children that know an amazing number of facts, they know the capital of Romania, and they know all kinds of other facts, but they still are amazingly stupid. They can't string it together and think.' To get beyond that will require breakthroughs in the area of artificial general intelligence, a contentious field that certainly has its optimists but where many experts doubt serious progress is imminent. As Yoav Shoham, professor emeritus at Stanford and one of the world's leading AI researchers, has said, 'I often like to have this picture in mind, it's a cartoon I saw when I was young, of a kid standing – looking at the stars – with a telescope but standing on a little chair to get closer to the stars. And, that's what AI is. The stars are intelligence. The chair is current-day AI machine learning.' While in the view of Steve Furber, professor of computer engineering at the University of Manchester, 'For a full-scale computer model of the human brain, we'd be looking at a machine that would need to be housed in an aircraft hangar and consume tens of megawatts.' It would, he has said, 'need a small power station just to keep it going.'

The notion of a world where machines seamlessly replace humans, rendering whole industries and job categories obsolete, is probably too neat a picture. Much more likely is that artificial intelligence and

machine learning will become more and more prevalent over time, but deployed alongside people rather
than in preference to them. We have a head of AI
whose job is to identify opportunities to automate
processes in our business, but that doesn't mean we
are laying people off as a result. Automation doesn't
have to be a zero-sum game where it is one machine
in and one human out. It can just as much be about
how to optimise the business model you already have,
helping people to do their jobs better or to improve
the customer experience.

That's not to say many of today's jobs won't cease
to exist in time. But that in itself is nothing new, and
nothing that hasn't happened in countless cycles over
the centuries. Just as it is a near certainty that many
aspects of the current labour market will become
obsolete, we can be fairly sure that there are going
to be new jobs, or new versions of existing jobs. Every
generation spawns new tools and technologies that
create employment around them. Once a month, I
have a lunch in the Simply Business office where
anyone can come along and have a chat. At one of
the recent ones, I worked out that about 7 out of 10
jobs around the table wouldn't have existed when I
started my career: UX designer, digital product lead
and social media manager among them.

As anyone who was made to sit one of those
computer-driven career surveys at school will know,
we tend to get more wrong about the future of work
than right. I was apparently destined to become a
tank driver, which disappointingly still hasn't happened

(and with the advent of the self-driving tank, probably never will).

So don't be too surprised if we're still having discussions, writing books and making documentaries about automation in another 40 years' time. There are plenty of examples of extreme progress that could lead you to the assumption that human workers are going the way of the dodo. Though for every handy-looking robot that has its unblinking eye on your job, there is a supermarket self-checkout machine that can't detect unexpected onions in the bagging area, let alone determine without human help whether you are legally entitled to booze and fags.

Nobody can turn around and say with confidence what jobs are going to continue to exist, in what volume, for what length of time. While my instinct is that the most headline-grabbing predictions about automaton are simplistic and overblown, there are so many unknowable factors that it would be naive to rule out such scenarios. Which means the most important question, and the one with which I want to conclude, is what can we do to start preparing for the upheaval, whenever and in whatever degree it may come?

CHAPTER 9

FOUR DAYS A WEEK

'From the moment when the machine first made its appearance it was clear to all thinking people that the need for human drudgery, and therefore to a great extent for human inequality, had disappeared. If the machine were used deliberately for that end, hunger, overwork, dirt, illiteracy, and disease could be eliminated within a few generations.'

In *1984* George Orwell gives those words to Emmanuel Goldstein, leader of the resistance against the totalitarian state. In Orwell's dystopia, the potential of technology to create a more prosperous and equal society has been frustrated; the powerful instead concentrate on the question of 'how to keep the wheels of industry turning without increasing the real wealth of the world', preventing the prosperity that might threaten their position from spreading to the masses.

Orwell was writing in 1949, almost two decades after the economist John Maynard Keynes had offered a more hopeful perspective on the same theme. In his 1930 essay, 'Economic Possibilities for our Grandchildren', he looked forward to a time, a century later, when 'there will be ever larger and larger classes and groups of people from whom problems of economic necessity have been practically removed.' By 2030, he suggested, we could be enjoying 'an age of leisure and abundance', with work occupying perhaps no more than 15 hours a week, made possible by advances in technology.

Whether from a hopeful or cynical standpoint, the power of machines to liberate people from the necessity of work has long been discussed and written about. Yet despite the huge advances in technology, and the reduction in working hours that has taken place over the long term, freedom from Orwell's 'drudgery' and Keynes's 'necessity' seems no closer than it was when they were writing.

In the face of fast-advancing automation, this is a debate we need to return to. Many existing jobs may become redundant, but does that not also create the opportunity to realise what the potential of technology has always been: to allow people to work less and to enjoy a life that does not have to revolve around the economic necessity of full-time work?

Pie in the sky, you might think, given so many people report they are working more not less.

However, it speaks to a question that we need to ask ourselves as the realities of automation start to become clear. Should our response be about trying to recreate the existing model of work in a more technological world, or is there potential for a more radical reboot where we embrace the power of technology rather than fearing it?

Instead of being merely responsive to the progress of artificial intelligence in the workplace, paring away jobs as they are no longer required, companies have an opportunity to be more proactive in how they prepare themselves and their people for this potentially dramatic moment of change.

In the face of a change whose speed, scale and direction are unclear, we need an experimental approach to start modelling what a new way of working might look like, and ultimately how we can move towards it. One such idea, which we have now implemented on a trial basis at Simply Business, is the 4-day working week, something we are now testing and plan to roll out across our whole contact-centre team by 2020.

We are doing this because we believe it can be good for our employees, a boost to wellbeing and productivity, and good for our business. The basic premise is: if you don't actually need people to work a 5-day week to deliver the required business results, why make them? In our contact centre, technology is creating efficiencies that can automate some of the processes we previously relied on people for, from collecting customer-satisfaction data to helping direct customers to relevant products. We believe that the aggregate effect of these efficiencies can make a shorter working week possible, without hurting business performance. Our hypothesis is also that they can pay for it, meaning we will keep wages the same while asking people to work only four days.

It's definitely the case that technological efficiencies of this kind will create a dividend, and the question then becomes how you choose to invest it. If realising value for shareholders was our only aim, we would probably be taking every opportunity to automate these jobs and return the savings to our ownership. That would inevitably mean redundancies.

We don't want to do that, and not just because eliminating people's jobs for the enrichment of shareholders is as morally dubious a position as it sounds. There is also a commercial reality that cuts squarely across the notion that automation should be used as a cost saver, pure and simple. That is – presuming you're still a business that is still going to be employing some people – you need people to want to work for you, and to work well. And if there is one way to kill morale, loyalty and productivity in your business, it is to make those who keep their jobs watch on as many of their colleagues lose theirs.

Instead we are experimenting to try and answer two questions. Can we, through automating some processes in the contact centre, deliver the same or better results with fewer human hours worked? And in parallel, without cutting either the number of people or their pay, can we maintain a sustainable business model?

A lot of companies have introduced flexible working schemes that move in this direction but stop short of actually letting people work less while earning the same. Some, like the parent company of Japanese retailer Uniqlo, offer staff the option of working 4 longer days of 10 hours, rather than 5 of 8 hours. Others, such as Amazon, have offered deals where people can go down to a 30-hour week but receive only 75 per cent of their pay. I don't believe in doing either of those things: longer hours, given their links to stress and long-term health problems, are a dangerous thing for any employer to encourage. Nor does it seem right to create a new normal of lower wages apart from those who already choose to work part-time. The objective is not to re-engineer the working week but to actually reduce it, experimenting directly with the question of whether technology can allow people to work less on a basis that is economically sustainable for both the business and the individual. So we are trying the full-fat version of the shorter week: 4 shifts of 8 hours – a 32-hour week – and exactly the same pay packet as before. The metric we are looking at is a simple one: total employment costs divided by earned revenue. If we can keep that stable or improve it, then we will know that – in terms of the business case, at least – the experiment is working.

At the moment this is just an experiment and one in its early days. It could fail if the technology doesn't deliver the productivity gains we hope for, if unforeseen inefficiencies in the new system become apparent, or it seems like we have ceded advantage to one of our competitors.

But we are making it our central programme for exploring what a future model of work might look like, for a number of reasons. We reckon there is a productivity benefit, one that will be good for the business as well as for our people; we think there are human and environmental advantages to removing an unnecessary day's work, if it indeed proves to be unnecessary; and finally we believe that freeing up more time is one of the most important ways to help people start preparing for a future where their current job is less likely to exist. Ultimately, we think the current model is unsustainable, and it is only going to become more so over time. The 4-day week is an experiment that, even if it does not prove to be the end point, should help us to work our way towards new answers and a more effective model. Moreover, there are some good reasons to believe it will deliver tangible benefits in our business right now, and for our team as they look towards their future careers.

Benefits right now

'Better work gets done in four days than five,' the technology entrepreneur Jason Fried wrote in 2012. At his software company, now called Basecamp, he operates a seasonal 4-day week policy that runs annually from May to October. 'When there's less time to work, you waste less time. When you have a compressed workweek, you tend to focus on what's important.'

This is one of the most obvious potential benefits of the shorter working week. Anyone who has ever done a day's work in an office knows how much time gets wasted; it's humanly impossible to be switched on and doing productive work day after day without losing a little, and often a lot, of time to the many distractions technology and the Internet now offer us. A study of Dutch call centre workers by the Institute of Labor Economics found that there were only 4.6 effective hours of work per day on average. Could a shorter week, and the promise of more time away from the office, help focus minds? Some of the evidence from early trials of the shorter week is promising.

One of the most high-profile experiments took place in 2008, when Utah Governor Jon Huntsman enacted a change to the working conditions of the state's public-sector workers. Instead of doing 5 days of 8 hours each week, they would do 4 days of 10. The policy, which was conceived as a budgetary measure in the teeth of the financial crisis, actually ended up spreading goodwill more effectively than it cut costs. Annual savings from the closure of public buildings yielded only a third of the expected amount. But among the state's workers, the approach was hugely popular. It ended after three years with approval ratings of 85 per cent, while two-thirds of people said it made them work more productively, absenteeism reduced, and the non-availability of public services dropped to zero. People also noted the savings on one day's worth of commuting a week.

Some small-scale experiments with the four-day week have also shown it can form part of a successful business model. The UK design agency Normally started giving its team Fridays off in 2017, and reported that it more than doubled its revenues in the first year with shorter working weeks.

While the evidence on the benefits of shorter hours is still nascent at company level, there is an established link at a macro level between lower hours and higher productivity. OECD statistics show there is a clear correlation between countries where longer hours are the norm – such as Greece, Poland and Estonia – and lower productivity. The hypothesis that people will work more efficiently in a shorter week may be yet to be comprehensively proven, but it seems an obvious and important one to test, especially when it is not just a question of people doing the same work in fewer hours, but being able to lean on technology to pick up some of the slack.

In addition to improving productivity, the shorter working week has the potential to improve the well-being and job satisfaction of the team. An extra day can free up time to meet pressing family needs that are often difficult to balance against full-time work, whether that is childcare or looking after elderly parents. And it can give people the time, whether to learn a new skill or simply put their feet up, that so many increasingly feel is lacking in their lives. When

Durham University conducted a global survey of over 18,000 people across 134 countries, more than two-thirds said they felt they didn't get enough rest, to do things like reading, being in the natural environment or simply being alone.

Professor John Ashton, who was president of the Faculty of Public Health in the UK between 2013 and 2016, has said that a 4-day week could help counteract trends including the growing prevalence of work-related mental health problems and other health issues linked to overwork. 'We need a 4-day week so that people can enjoy their lives, have more time with their families, and maybe reduce high blood pressure because people might start exercising on that extra day,' he told the *Guardian* in 2014. A 2-year experiment in Sweden, in which some nurses in a Gothenburg elderly care home worked 6-hour days, suggested health benefits to a shorter working week. Nurses in the control group, who continued to work 8-hour days, took 62.5 per cent more sick days than those in the 6-hour trial group.

Employers who have instituted a shorter working week have also spoken about the benefits to employee morale and wellbeing. As Sat Bains, the 2-Michelin star chef who has been operating a 4-day week in his restaurants for the past few years, has said: 'The guys can't wait to come to work because they feel fresh. They can't wait to start performing at this level because we've invested in them. By showing them we give a shit, and we care about their time off and their livelihood and their leisure and family time, we've shown a commitment.'

Beyond productivity and wellbeing, there are also environmental benefits of the shorter week to be considered. The Utah 4-day experiment saw the state government's carbon emission 5 reduce by 14 per cent. The aggregate level of car journeys saved and, where relevant, offices closed could combine to have a significant impact on the environmental burden that business creates.

The benefits of the shorter working week are in the process of being proven. It is not a panacea that will be directly applicable for every business or indeed every worker. Plenty of experiments with a shorter working week have been tried and failed: Treehouse, a Portland-based online education company, reverted to the 5-day week after a redundancy round, while the Gothenburg experiment with 6-hour days was not continued after the local government concluded it would cost too much to implement.

But although the economic model and the tangible benefits in productivity and wellbeing still require more evidence to support them, the opportunity is clear. With long hours having become the norm, and stress- and work-related mental health issues on the rise, a shorter working week could be part of the answer as to how we make work less onerous for people, and more productive for companies. It is one of the ways that technology can be utilised to the mutual benefit of both companies and people.

Benefits to come

If a 4-day week is one way we might realise the benefits of automation in business as it stands, it can also create space to help companies and their employees prepare for the working world that automation will create in the next decade.

It is now the duty of an employer to be honest with their employees about the nature of the uncertainty we face. At least some, and possibly many, of the jobs that exist today will not in the short- to medium-term future. Companies need to both recognise this and work with their people on what it means for them.

At a moment when there is so much upheaval about to hit employment norms, I think it is the basic moral obligation of employers to help and support those who are most likely to be affected by this change. Not all would agree with this. In early 2017, I was at an entrepreneurs' conference where a senior executive from Uber was speaking. During the Q&A, I recounted a conversation I'd recently had with an Uber driver, who when I asked him what he thought about self-driving technology and what it would mean for him, said he didn't realise that Uber was one of the companies working hardest to try and develop it. What, I asked the executive, did Uber see as its social obligation to these drivers, to help them prepare for this coming dislocation? His answer, in blunt terms, was that they didn't have one; if Uber wasn't going to invest in this technology, someone else would, and it wasn't Uber's problem if some people were going to lose out as a result. In fairness that was under the previous CEO and the culture may since have changed. But it outlines that employers face a choice – whether to simply look out for their own interests when it comes to the disruption automation will cause, or to also do what they can to help their people get ready.

I think the most useful and honest thing you can say to people is that they are almost certainly going to need new skills, and need to start thinking about what they might do in a future where their current job ceases to exist, even if that is not imminent.

This is another area in which the shorter week can come into its own, by creating the space to help people both think about that future and work on the skills and experience that can help equip them for it. As part of our 4-day week experiment, we are going to give our people opportunities to do exactly that. We are bringing life coaches into the business who can talk to them about what their future options might be and how they can go about achieving them. We are subsidising skills training for those who want it, to learn about areas of work they may not encounter in the next year or few but almost certainly will at some point in the next decade and beyond. For example, a number of our contact centre team have started to train as product managers, with the prospect of moving to our London office and joining that side of the business. We are going to do the same for those who want to consider becoming developers. Others may want to train in entirely unrelated fields, and that is something we will support in the same way.

People can use the extra day however they want, whether that is to spend more time with their family, reduce the cost of childcare, or just sit on the sofa and read or play Xbox all day. We're not going to monitor or track what people do: it's their time, and that is a fundamental part of the bargain. But we are going to put in place facilities and programmes that allow people to use that time, if they so choose, to undertake training and development that can help them move to another job that might have a lower propensity to automation.

Even if you don't believe it is a company's responsibility to help its people prepare for what their future jobs might be, there is a good commercial reason to take this approach, because if your employees need new skills for a changing world, then so does your business. If we can create an internal pipeline of software developers, and save on what are significant recruitment costs to find external candidates, then that serves our business need as well as helping support individual career futures.

It's an approach that large corporates such as AT&T are starting to take: since 2013 it has invested $250m in training around half of its 280,000-strong workforce for tech-related roles it increasingly needs to fill. Employees can use an internal platform to look at skills shortages and hiring trends in the company, and decide what role they would like to pursue, with most of the training done through online courses. No one would argue with that, but you also have to create the time and space for people to make changes such as this, and I don't think that's possible within the structure of the existing working week, or through the occasional stretch of paid leave.

Through the 4-day week, therefore, we are not just seeking to improve people's experience of work, and fight back against the problems of overwork and stress. We also want to give people the space and time to prepare for the future that is on the way, where we cannot rely on the jobs of today remaining viable.

***

When 2030 arrives, I very much doubt that we will be enjoying the 15-hour working week that Keynes prophesied. But I do think we need to recapture some of the ideas that he proposed, and to focus not just on the threats that technology poses to existing jobs, but the opportunity that it offers to reboot our basic mode of work, one that is neither fit for the present nor sustainable into the future.

Despite the fears that exist about the impact automation will have on jobs, there is no inevitability that workers will get left on the scrapheap, as collateral damage in the march of the machines. Instead there is a perfectly viable path that says a business can invest in its people, focus on maximising the value of the uniquely human contribution they can bring (whether that is brilliant, empathetic customer service; lateral thinking around a difficult problem; or creative excellence), and make adjustments accordingly. There is nothing to say that you cannot pay people the same to do less work, and that they cannot deliver equivalent or even greater value as a result.

It comes down to what you want to measure: inputs or outputs, hours worked or meaningful work delivered and value created. If you start measuring people by what they actually achieve, and stop worrying about when or where they do it, or how long it takes, then an entirely different equation becomes possible. At the moment we are still hooked on paying people to turn up, and all the assumptions and structures follow from it; in the world we are entering, that mindset needs to shift to rewarding people for what they meaningfully contribute. Businesses are going to have to get used to paying the same or more money for fewer hours. None of which means they cannot get more value, and make a bigger profit as a result. It just means we need to reassess the value we place on human labour, and the cost calculations that underpin it.

This reboot in our thinking also needs to extend to what the purpose of work is, as well as how it is practised. We know that lack of personal fulfilment is another of the problems endemic in work today. According to a Hay Group study, only 15 per cent of UK workers consider themselves to be 'highly motivated' in their work, while just 17 per cent said they were in their 'dream job'. As the author Yuval Noah Harari has said, 'We really need to protect the humans, not the jobs. The crisis here is a crisis of meaning not of employment. If you can solve the crisis of meaning then you can forget about jobs.'

Automation could help counteract this, making large parts of the work that people find demotivating the domain of machines, not least what GE among others has defined as the 'dull, dangerous and dirty' jobs. We should see this as a good thing, as long as alternatives can be found. None of us grew up dreaming of picking parcels in a warehouse or formatting numbers on a spreadsheet. That is not to demean or discredit any of the jobs that exist today but to be frank about admitting that some can be unfulfilling and lack meaning. I've done jobs like that, and I certainly didn't feel I had climbed very far up Maslow's hierarchy when I was doing them. We need to shed fewer tears about the jobs that are going to be lost, many of which the machines are frankly welcome to. And we need to focus more on how people can be helped to find work that is both less susceptible to AI and more personally fulfilling.

The onus must be on creating work that is both more human and more humanising: reliant less on the repetitive performance of tasks and more on creative, emotional and communication skills. That may mean we need to re-evaluate our perception of what type of work is most economically and socially valuable. A growing, ageing population means more pressure on both the education and social care systems, two areas of the economy that perennially face recruitment problems and where pay hardly reflects the social value of the work.

While education, at least, is a profession that should be well insulated from automation, given the importance of the human interaction. It is jobs such as these, left behind by the market forces of recent decades, that could become newly desirable, as emerging technology wipes out employment that is better paid and more sought after.

In the end, the fundamental question is how the dividends of automation are going to be used. Returning all value to the bottom line is the utilitarian option, but one that threatens to trash the credibility of your business, and any hope of establishing a meaningful culture among the people that remain. Instead, companies should think about investing those proceeds in more meaningful jobs and roles for their people, which can in turn deliver greater value for the business when harnessed alongside effective use of technology.

It may be technology driving change and uncertainty, but it is businesses that have the power to help determine what the outcome of that change will be. A dystopian, machine-dominated future is possible; but so too is one in which the virtues of the human mind are allied to the power of machine intelligence. Where we end up will be in a large part determined by the choices that businesses make, and the world companies collectively invest in creating. The challenge is to elevate the role and purpose of the work that people do, to make the most of our advantages as humans in a world increasingly defined by automation.

The machines may be coming, but it is the companies that encourage greater autonomy, while they automate, that stand the best chance of thriving. Business needs a plan for human potential as much as a strategy for artificial intelligence. There is every reason to hope, and expect, that the march of the machines can also spark a rise of the people: into more fulfilling work, more meaningful careers, and ultimately more enjoyable, healthier lives.

CONCLUSION

REASONS TO BE CHEERFUL

Although most people who start and run companies are optimists by nature, there has perhaps been a tendency recently for the debate surrounding business to become fatalistic: the robots are coming for all the jobs; big tech is coming for all our businesses; trust is being lost and it isn't coming back.

Business undoubtedly has its challenges, and must move more decisively to address them. Our current operating model, one designed for the norms of the 20th century, needs a reboot if it is to be ready for the change that lies ahead.

I believe companies can and will address the issues that I outlined at the beginning of this book and which, if ignored, threaten to undermine both long-term business performance and public and political trust in business. There is both growing momentum around movements for more ethical, transparent and long-term minded business (such as B Corp), and growing pressure from consumers, employees, regulators and politicians alike for companies to move on from some of the old malpractices. The imperative for change is growing, as the opportunities to be gained by embracing it are becoming more apparent.

Business can adapt to the change that surrounds it on all sides, by not being wowed or cowed by the progress of technology; but instead maintaining an unerring focus on the needs of customers at all times, and leaving behind the rigid plan–and–deliver model of old in favour of a more experimental approach that aligns the opportunities of what technology can deliver to the realities of what customers actually want.

It can rebuild trust by showing willingness to embrace the broader set of responsibilities that a more complex and transparent world demands: to not just provide products and services, but actively champion and safeguard customer needs; to not just be an employer but a nurturer of people's careers; and to see environmental and social concerns not as marginal but as an essential part of everyday business thinking.

And it can counteract the growing crisis of engagement and meaning in the workplace, by ditching the legacy of scientific management in favour of an approach that gives people autonomy and control over their working lives, and recognises the complexity of what motivates us by moving beyond the reliance on financial incentives. In turn, the 'time is money' mindset needs to go, and be replaced by an acceptance that it is what people deliver that matters, not the hours they put in. Fifteen productive hours in a week beats 50 low-output ones; working arrangements need to be re-valued accordingly.

A critical mass of companies who think and behave in this way – building more productive, responsible and human businesses that experiment their way into the future – can have a meaningful impact on many of the pressing socio-economic issues we face: from the instability of unemployment to pressure on the environment, income inequality and the mental and physical strain of overwork. Better business can make a meaningful difference; and it can do better business at the same time. Surrounded by uncertainty, business needs to give up on many of its old certainties: in this landscape, it is the unstructured organisation that can adapt quicker to emerging trends and technologies; the self-organising business that can put experiments in place at the pace they need to happen; and the informal culture that allows ideas and decisions to flow freely in all directions. In a more technological age, companies need to be organised less like machines, and more in ways that allow the messier, unpredictable but imaginative power of the human perspective to come to the fore.

When there is so much focus (quite rightly) on change, companies also need to remember that some fundamentals have stayed the same. Customers are still customers, marketing is still marketing, and a good employer is still a good employer. I have called for a reboot and not a wholesale reinvention, because the essentials of good business remain what they always have been: to identify a real customer need, to find better, faster and more affordable ways of meeting that need than your competitors, and to be a place where people want to come and do their best work.

The end point hasn't really changed, but the means to achieve it constantly are changing, and the demands being put on business as they do are in turn much greater. So as companies look towards the change surrounding them and their industries, they need to remember the essential continuities even while embracing the need for a new model and more effective organising principles.

As well as acknowledging continuities, we need to recognise the choices that every business has. Technology is sometimes spoken of as if it is an irrepressible tide, but the reality is we have choices about how we use technology and, just as important, distribute the dividends realised as a result.

If a business wants to use technology to maximise every possible efficiency and return all the gains to shareholders, then nobody is going to stop them. But it is hard to think that increasingly preference – in the eyes of customers, employees and indeed investors – will not move towards businesses who take a more holistic, responsible approach: investing the gains of technology and change in everything from the future prospects of their people to more environmentally friendly ways of doing business and better products and services for customers.

Everything I have talked about in this book is within the power of individual companies and leaders to control. No business is a hostage to change or fortune, or obligated to continue with the broken model of old. We can shape the business environment and working world we want to exist. That does not have to mean inevitable trade-offs or painful compromises. In fact, if the necessity of a reboot is grasped, there is every reason to believe the future our children inherit will be one not just where technology abounds, but where companies prosper and people thrive.

Acknowledgements

This book would not have been possible without the support of Josh Davis. Your help in structuring the argument and developing the ideas has been critical and I am indebted to you for all of your partnership, and for introducing me to the word shibboleth. I will think of you every time it comes up and then google its meaning. It's been a joy working with you, Josh, so thank you.

Likewise, the encouragement, wise words and support from Nick Giles and the whole team at Seven Hills has been greatly appreciated. Nick, I just hope this sells as well as *Mission*. Sincere thanks also to Joel Rickett at Penguin Random House for your support of the project from day one and your editorial guiding hand, and to the team at Virgin Books.

This work is the product of the many conversations, debates and experiences from all the businesses I have been involved in over the past 20 years and more. So to everyone I have worked with, at Trailfinders, last-minute.com, Match.com, Skyscanner, the Drinkaware

Trust and, of course, Simply Business, thank you. Everything I've talked about in this book is fundamentally a product of the mistakes I've made and the lessons I've learned. I am still a work in progress. And I can only apologise if you got the younger version of me.

Particular thanks go to the brilliant team at Simply Business. This book is your story as much as anyone's, a product of all the ideas, insights and endeavours of hundreds of people over the last eight years. I hope you all feel as proud as I do of what we have created, and that this book helps document some of your many achievements. Thank you for all of your hard work, goodwill and support. It is appreciated more than I can say.

Profound thanks to Chris Slater, who has been my partner and inspiration in building the business. He is without a doubt the best person I have ever worked with and has made me want to be worthy of being a CEO. Likewise, Lukas Oberhuber, who is not only a friend but has the unique ability as a CTO to be both visionary and practical in equal measure. Most of the best ideas in our business have come from him, usually about two years before I realised he was right. Fiona McSwein has not only supported the book project from start to finish but continues to inspire me with her optimism, intellect and passion. Neil Edwards provided typically candid and insightful feedback on early drafts.

Thanks also to Arvinder 'Harvey' Mangat, who through the early days was always a force for good in everything we tried to achieve and helped me shape the values of the business that exists today. Also Kevin 'Flembo' Fleming, the least likely CFO I have ever met and whose work ethic and eternal good humour is second only to his encyclopaedic knowledge of wine. I wanted to acknowledge how instrumental you both were in the early years of creating SB.

Thanks to Dr Keith O'Brien, who has been hugely influential in bringing behavioural science alive for the whole business, and gave invaluable input into the ideas presented here; to David Summers, the most natural and obvious CEO there has ever been; and to other key members of the UK team: Sarah Haigh, Deborah Holland, Alan Thomas, Laura Winter, Kelly Harris, Bea Montoya, Phil Williams, Stewart Duncan, Louis Badcock, Paul Comley. I am so proud to call all of you colleagues and friends.

To Bill, Santosh, Illyse, Pat, Eric and the US team, I am inspired and privileged to witness the business you are creating and I am greatly looking forward to the success you will have over the coming years.

Special thanks to the work of Tracey Hibble and Sarah Grealy who quite frankly make the world work in a way that makes sense. For all of your support and help over the years, a huge thank you.

I also want to thank and remember the late Robin Gilkes, who was one of the main reasons I joined the business in the first place and who was a steadying force in many of our more difficult moments early on. To Robin's family, I want you to know how much he was loved and respected by us all.

To Alan Schnitzer, Greg Toczydlowski, AJ Kess and Lisa Caputo I want to say a special thanks for your friendship and your support on this project. For everyone at Travelers who has made us all feel so welcome, I wanted to say how much it is appreciated, particularly the friendship and support of Kevin Smith.

To Brent Hoberman and Martha Lane Fox – for all of the imperfections of lastminute.com, it remains the founding inspiration for the ideas that have been the basis of this book. You taught me that work can be fun, that businesses don't have to be hierarchical and that informality and ambition are not mutually exclusive. For that, and all your support, I am eternally grateful.

I'm indebted to Tim O'Reilly and Douglas Rushkoff, whose ideas and thinking have been instrumental in shaping my views on business and technology. Thank you for your time and support on this project, and I hope it does you proud. Charles Wookey at the Blueprint for Better Business also kindly made time to discuss some of the ideas here and to share his expertise.

Special thanks to Toby and Debbie Hill for their feedback and comments, to Lea Simpson and MT Rainey for their always stimulating advice and to Tim Wheeler for his thoughtful comments on the early draft. To my friends and forum mates in YPO: Jim Hall, Cameron Chartouni, Craig Cesman, Marc

Meyohas, Peter Jackson, Rima Hall and Chris Bowden. Our conversations have changed the course of my life in a positive way and I am grateful and appreciative of your friendship and support.

Thanks also to David Kelly who has over the years been a boss, chairman and inspiration for me. Challenging, practical and empathetic in equal measure, always great fun to be around and without a doubt the best example how success and humility can go hand in hand.

To Dan Britton, quite simply the best friend I could ever wish for. Your optimism and good humour are not natural and I love you for that. You do need to carry out a 'fact checker', though, to calibrate some of your more strident opinions. I'm glad you are so physically repulsive otherwise you would be perfect.

I also wanted to recognise my teachers at Waltham Tollbar school back in the late 1980s. There were a number of teachers that looked out for me in ways that went above and beyond, especially Margaret Peaty and Alan Boxall. You probably didn't realise it at the time, but your example and support meant a great deal to me.

And finally to my family. To my mum and brothers Simon, Nathan and Ashley, thanks for the constant love, laughter and for keeping it real over the years. A bit too real sometimes when sharing bedrooms on our annual brothers' trip. To Lindsey, John, Kate and Anna, from the first time we met, when I fell off a broken chair and Lindsey snorted her drink over me, thanks for making me feel part of the family.

To Bryn, who is quite simply the father I never had, and Margaret, who is the best grandmother children could wish for, thank you for making me part of the Butler family. And most importantly, to Toby, Yenna, Lottie, Jack, Will and Poppy, I am confident the future is bright with you all in charge. I love you all.

The real inspiration for this book has been my children, Bea and Tom. Since you came into our lives you have made me think every day of how I can make you proud and help create a space in the world for you to be the brilliant people you are becoming. Bea, you are kind, funny, smart, beautiful and creative in ways I could only hope to be. Tom, your sense of warmth, humour, intelligence, imagination and speed of thought amaze me. The world makes sense with you two in it and you are and will always be my greatest achievement in life. I love being your dad; it's by far the best and most challenging job I've ever had and I hope I am the father you both deserve.

To Lorna, my partner in everything, the love of my life. For helping me realise the true meaning of kindness and trust, which is the foundation from which everything is possible. I'm so glad we found each other and for all of your support, guidance and love over the years. I am excited about what we are building together and I hope this work makes you proud and optimistic about the years to come as we love, learn and continue to build our lives together. I am not poetic enough to do justice to how much I love you, but John Berger was:

What reconciles me to my own death more than anything else is the image of a place: a place where your bones and mine are buried, thrown, uncovered, together. They are strewn there pell-mell. One of your ribs leans against my skull. A metacarpal of my left hand lies inside your pelvis. (Against my broken ribs your breast like a flower.) The hundred bones of our feet are scattered like gravel. It is strange that this image of our proximity, concerning as it does mere phosphate of calcium, should bestow a sense of peace. Yet it does. With you I can imagine a place where to be phosphate of calcium is enough.

John Berger – *And our Faces, My Heart, Brief as Photos*